free

Feeling

REAL

Emotions

Everyday

by
Pearl Howie

First Edition
Copyright © Pearl Howie 2016
All rights reserved
ISBN 978-0-9956474-0-4
The moral right of the author has been asserted

With unconditional love and hugs to
all the people in my life who tried to protect me,
tried to teach me,
tried to love me,
but most of all to the ones
who helped me to be wild and free.

Contents

Safety Advice	6
Preface	8
Introduction	12
free - Feeling Real Emotions Everyday	17
I Ran Away From Home When I Was Just A Child	24
Unconditional Love	36
Numbing	41
Letting Go of My Pride	43
Knowing Not Thinking (Road Closed)	46
The Love Of My Life	49
Native Healing	54
Leave My Mystery Alone	60
Leave My Money Alone	63
Leave My Body Alone	69
I Don't Have To Like Myself	72
I Am An Eagle	75
Why I Hate Being Grateful	79
Self-Imposed Slavery	82
Shoulds – Warning Lights (It Shouldn't Bother Me When)	87
It Is Given	88
Teach What You Need	92
Helping Others	93
Pissing People Off	98
Feeling Worthless	99
Leave My Success Blocks Alone	102

Going Against Yourself For Love	104
Going Against Yourself For Happiness	108
Bad Habits – What Is Acceptable Now Will Be Illegal Tomorrow (and Vice Versa)	113
Destiny	117
I Can Be Wrong – It's Safe To Make Mistakes	118
The Wilful Suspension of Disbelief	120
What Do Stars Do – They Shine	123
I Don't Care	124
Waking Others Up	127
Positive Thinking and Forgiving My Teachers	128
Listen To Your Heart	134
P.S.	135
Photo Credits	142
About the Author	142
Other Titles by the Author	143
Book References and Further Reading	144

Safety Advice

Dear Fellow Traveller,

A word of caution before you enter this book. Take it at your own pace.

Since I fell in love with massage in 2009 I've explored over two hundred unique practices and many other escapes. I've had emergency medical treatment several times, twice for pedicures gone wrong and one I'll tell you about in a moment. I've been dehydrated, scarred, been left beaten and bruised and, of course, got lost.

I've also taught thousands of fitness classes and had various sporting injuries. I almost never have anyone have an injury in my class - we always warm up. We have a saying "any movement is good" because the chance of serious injury is so slight compared to the benefits of any exercise. When you get in tune with your body, you learn when to slow down, drink more water, walk it out or just stop, and then it's even easier. You learn when it's safe to take three steps forward and when you need to just take one.

I've been blessed to have worked with some amazing healers, with traditions handed down through generations for thousands of years. They know how to do these things safely. The maximum amount of massage recommended at a time is two hours. I've also had an experienced healer shake their head at the massage I had chosen and tell me "No, you can't take that – let's do this instead."

I had no hesitation in experiencing a traditional sweat lodge in Mexico, but I know people have died in other sweat lodges. I loved fire walking but I know that people have been burned when attempting other fire walks.

The most common cause of death in the US is now overdose on prescription medication, including painkillers and anti-depressants. Our modern way of life is killing us as surely as our modern diet. It's not working. But when we try to reconnect with our ancient wisdom we have to be careful to treat that with respect and patience.

I have a book by my bed about native American healing. It has a warning about using herbs without proper understanding and cites an example of a women's group poisoning themselves when on a detox. The other night I decided to make a blend of essential oils. So much better for me than a chemical air freshener, right? I woke up a few hours later, my lungs burning (thank goodness the windows were open). A call to an emergency helpline and I was advised to get down to the hospital to be properly checked out. I'm okay but still recovering.

The chemicals in herbs, plants and essential oils are just as potent as in a tablet, and just as deadly.

You cannot get fit in one day. You cannot grieve in one day. I once went to a five star spa thinking "Wow, this will be like having a week's holiday in a day". Then could barely stay awake for the next week. There's a reason we need to take time out.

When you open the door to feeling your real emotions it can be a lot to handle. One step at a time is great progress. This is not a quick fix. This is a practice. It doesn't happen overnight (unlike asphyxiating yourself). For the best practical guide to personal freedom please read "The Four Agreements" which is wisdom that is thousands of years old. This book and my other books are just my experience of discovering ancient wisdom from my modern perspective.

Freedom can be scary and dangerous. Leaving a life where you know the rules can feel like descending into chaos. We yearn for freedom and then it terrifies us. People who are released from institutions, whether marriage, boarding school, prison or even concentration camps have experienced such difficulty in adapting back to "ordinary" life that they have returned, reoffended or even committed suicide.

It's hard for animals to adapt to being in the wild again (or in a safari park or reserve) when they're used to being kept in a cage, but it can be done. I believe we can adapt to freedom too, one step at a time.

Preface

To the love of my life,

I know you don't understand why it's important to me, to keep going back to the past, to the things that hurt me, to the times in my youth when I went numb, but I think you understand it too.

I survived.

Things happened in my life that were scary and beyond belief and beyond sad, things that could have killed me. Times I could have died by my own hand or others, I could have been an alcoholic or drug addict or a stripper in Vegas. I look back now and it hurts so much to see how close I was to death, how easy it would have been to miss out on all this, to have never even met you.

But the only way to survive the way I did was to let go of pieces of myself, to numb, to become someone else, like a secret agent in a war. A sleeper.

In the meantime I made my life amazing, sought out the best and most wonderful (darling that includes you, although you found me too), got so happy and met you and it was heaven. But it couldn't work, because you were meant for the real me and she wasn't here.

It is like the little mermaid, like I made a deal with the sea witch to give up a part of me, my voice and my tail, not so I could be with you, because I hadn't met you then, but so I could come up on dry land and survive the storm. And I forgot I was a mermaid (had to forget). I love to dance and that made up for not singing or swimming but a voice called to me from the sea – my voice. So I had to go back down to the very bottom of the ocean, because of you, and because of myself calling me back down, because I had to go back and rescue all the little pieces of me I had to leave behind in order to just survive, just stay in this life long enough to realise how wonderful it could be, long enough to meet you and see stars and the full moon and feel magic and moonlight and remember that we are perfect the day we are born and that I'm here now, learning to swim and sing again.

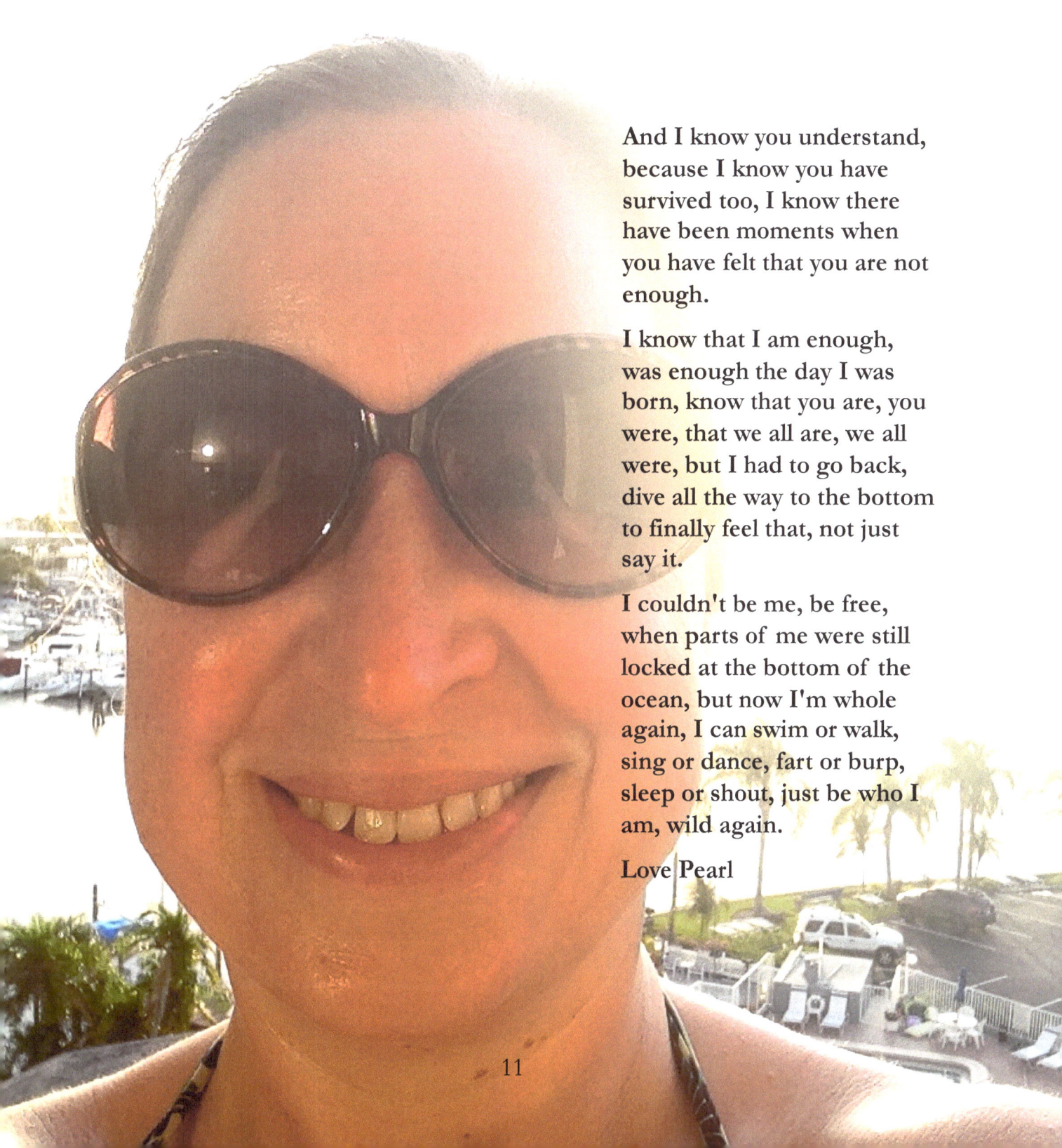

And I know you understand, because I know you have survived too, I know there have been moments when you have felt that you are not enough.

I know that I am enough, was enough the day I was born, know that you are, you were, that we all are, we all were, but I had to go back, dive all the way to the bottom to finally feel that, not just say it.

I couldn't be me, be free, when parts of me were still locked at the bottom of the ocean, but now I'm whole again, I can swim or walk, sing or dance, fart or burp, sleep or shout, just be who I am, wild again.

Love Pearl

Introduction

I thought about writing this book before I went on holiday (I got back yesterday), I thought I knew it, but when I was away I had an awakening, or rather a few small ones and then a massive bottom of the drawer (which I really hope is the last major one) awakening that has changed my life forever.

When I was writing my other books I always tried to write the truth as I knew it, as if I was writing to a good friend who needed my help – I didn't know I was writing to me.

And this book is for me as much as it is for you. It is a memory, like writing down a dream, although I think this is as real as it gets, so that I never, ever forget it again. In truth the moment I had the awakening it wasn't hard to stay with it, it was so raw and my feelings so powerful, like that movie you see that rocks your world, the kind you get to the end of and you have to watch it all over again because when you get that twist at the end it's like POW!... You'd made assumptions about everything and really the hero was the villain or the guy was dead and it's suddenly a different film. And now, guess what, it MAKES SENSE!!! Hallelujah! All those funny little bits, like, why did she go in there, that's crazy, when you watch it again it's like Aha! Yes, we talk about aha! moments, well, if you've ever been around any "spiritual" people (seriously, "spiritual" people, is that like "physical" people – you know, people with a body? Or "mental" people… Okay, we'll get into that…) And it can be so painful, when you realise the truth of your own life, it can feel like being punched in the gut.

What I learned on this journey is that 99% of what the world is telling you and you are telling yourself is bull crap. (Can you see I just came back from the United States? It's probably also going to take me a few weeks to get all the chemicals out of my system from the food I was eating – next time I am planning my trip around great experiences, hotels AND places that have organic food.) Oh yeah, and I can't resist bacon with buttermilk pancakes and maple syrup.

I've just started reading "Walden" by Henry David Thoreau, which was written in the early 1800s and he starts by talking about the things people told him he couldn't do, like live on vegetables or live away from others (he was planning to live alone as an experiment and I don't know what happens yet). It's a slow read because it's written in a more obtuse language and I keep falling asleep but it makes me laugh that he knew all this stuff way back then and we keep calling it New Age.

Many indigenous peoples knew it and know it and continue to know it, despite being looked down and despised by the very people they welcomed into their land; the colonials and missionaries who did such good work in treating the diseases they brought with them in the indigenous people it didn't kill off straight away.

The indigenous people from the jungle, the desert, the sea, the river, they know. And despite being moved from the land or taken from the land, despite being persecuted and segregated and rounded up and massacred, despite all this, most of them are willing to share it generously with those suffering from the sickness of being a modern man, suffering from being overloaded with information without wisdom.

Wow, this is going to be a fun book.

Why the hell would I write this? Because in awakening to myself I awaken to all the unhealed, hurting parts of me, I love myself warts and all. I have to suffer the consequences of my choices, own my own mistakes, as do we all, it's our shit. No one can feel our feelings for us.

In the words of Jesus from the Gospel of St Thomas: "If you bring forth what is within you, what you bring forth will save you. If you do not bring forth what it is within you, what you do not bring forth will destroy you."

free - Feeling Real Emotions Everyday

I made it up, the acronym.

I was trying to come up with a title for this book that conveyed everything inside; the heart of it. I knew it was about freedom, feeling free and then this acronym popped into my head and it's perfect.

And it's cyclical.

Feeling Real Emotions Everyday frees us and being free allows us to feel our real emotions everyday.

It takes time, great strength and understanding to allow all our feelings to come up - mind, body and spirit - spiritual pain is felt in the body, physical pain we deny is felt in the mind, it is all connected. Even now I'm untangling the real emotions from the false emotions. It is a practice to recognise the difference between grief and suffering.

We choose our own reality, our own dream, we can choose to transform our pain by either releasing it or realising it was something we just imagined.

Is it worth it? I think so, yes. Since my awakening I haven't taken a single painkiller or watched TV (okay, I do watch Grey's Anatomy box sets – but no adverts), I haven't had a single migraine (before I was having 1 or 2 a month) and the pain in my body is almost zero.

I have days when
I am on the
ceiling with joy,
or on the floor with sadness, but I am
releasing it or realising it is unfounded
– just made up by my pride and ego.

I'm unlearning what I've learned.

Loving ourselves does not mean pushing
through or rewarding ourselves or punishing ourselves, it just means taking the time to listen and remember how to make ourselves happy.

Every life coaching practice is designed to serve you, to help you change your own life, live your dream. It's meant to help, but sometimes it's the wrong thing or at the wrong time. I don't want to push you to exercise when you are sick or tired or when you would be better served by going for a long walk and hugging a tree or having a hot bath. I don't want to sell you a book that's not right for you.

Loving you means I want the best for you and more importantly I respect you enough to respect your dream of what is best for you. I am not here to fix anyone, puh… lease. (But I know that my pride will try to sneak back in and tell me I know best.)

So with that note to myself and to you, let me put my life coach hat on for a moment. I am trained and well read on the subject. Not that you should necessarily trust me, but know that I am doing my best to serve you in this moment. Are you free, alone, able to take some time for yourself?

How do you feel?

Remember, it took me years to finally come to a place where I could feel all of my feelings, and let go, be myself for the first time in decades. It's okay if you just stay with the feelings for a moment. It's okay if you decide you need to do this with a real person, find a therapist or a counsellor. It's okay if you are not ready for this today.

When I felt like I was losing my boyfriend last year I sat down and did this exercise. Luckily enough I found a secret bench in the middle of some bamboo. And I focused intensely on the feelings in my body (this is also called by some FOFBOC – feet on floor, bottom on chair) and I recognised something - the distress of feeling that someone I loved had changed, had become someone else, was not new. I went back to my college sweetheart, to the same pain, but it didn't stem from there. I went back and found the source, my brother's stroke at age 14. And I finally after 28 years I opened the door to my grief.

In Brené Brown's book "Rising Strong" I got to the end to find a note. It said her books were meant for use by, you know, the generally troubled, but if you suffered from Trauma or Complicated Grief you should seek professional help. I laughed – maybe the note should have been at the beginning of the book.

It was complicated grief, so complicated that when I spoke to my therapist she said "You know in 13 years you've never spoken about this." To which I shook my head, of course I had, hadn't I? It's amazing how we can deny our pain.

It's been a tough year. Every time I think I have grieved, released, moved on, I hit another grief pocket. In my native American healing when I started even to talk about it my body was wracked with strange pains, I couldn't breathe, I rocked, my muscles went into spasm. Grief is complicated I think even in the simplest of cases, but yes, my grief was extremely complicated.

How do you feel?

I understand now that I also felt guilty for grieving. The only way I can explain it is to imagine what it feels like to have had your child switched at birth. You love and adore your child, but you also ache for the missing years with another child. And it feels sacrilegious, as if you somehow love one more or less, but I know that it takes nothing from my relationship with my brother, who is my hero, who I have shared the most incredible journey with, to say that I have also missed out, have grieved for the lost years of hanging out in pubs with him, going to college with him, dismissing him as just my slightly annoying but adorable baby brother, travelling with him. And in amongst all that was grief for myself, for the teenage years that were suddenly the most grown up years of all. For having to put away being 16 and thoughtless, having to be responsible, to stop being myself.

In writing this book I realise it is not a straight line, not a single thread, it's more like a woven blanket or patchwork quilt, so as I tell it I unpull a belief from here, explain another aspect there, and hopefully by the end it all becomes clear. As they say, every story has a beginning, middle and an end, just not necessarily in that order.

How do you feel?

Are you ready to be real?

Are you ready to stop. Stop working, stop numbing, stop trying to fix the world, or fix dinner, or keep up with the laundry, or the neighbours, stop worrying about money, stop pretending to be anything other than yourself?

Are you ready even to sit down on the bathroom floor, with the laundry, ready to cry, ready to laugh, ready to feel your pain, your joy?

Are you ready to wake up to the pain in your body and heal it, rather than push it down with drugs or positive thinking? To listen to your need for sleep instead of caffeine, to your need for alone time rather than pleasing your friends or family?

Are you ready to stop blaming?

Are you ready to have patience with yourself, forgive yourself and others, know that you all did your best and stop suffering, stop punishing yourself for the past?

You have a choice in this moment. You are free. Free to choose what will make you happy, (that's truly happy, not numb). It may not be what makes me happy, or your brother or your sister or your mother or your father or your friends or society in general. The whole world may disagree with you.

(Remember you can start small, one step forward is great progress.)

There are many tools you can use to help you be a happy human, but I believe that you came to this book for something else. Because you didn't pick up one of the many books that promise to make you happy, you picked up a book called "free – Feeling Real Emotions Everyday".

This book is in service to you, to what you know you want to do, it is nothing more than a manual to help you change your mindset; to remember you are free.

If you get stuck, hug a tree, they are very wise and almost all friendly (you may get the odd bug bite and check for squirrels too). Or take your shoes off and walk on the grass, the sand, lay down on the grass and feel the earth.

You can listen to your body. You can use the Four Agreements, to just stop. To remember how it feels, how it felt when you were little, too young to be domesticated, to know when you needed to eat, to sleep, to be cuddled, to be fed, to be distracted or to be left alone to practise the difficult task of learning to walk for yourself. To just be you. The knowledge is still there inside you.

Or follow your heart and go somewhere, anywhere outside your comfort zone, follow your feet and let your body take you somewhere, to the right place for you. Many people travel to Sedona for the vortexes, the places of great energy so they say, (I didn't feel anything) but many wise people will also tell you "You are the vortex". Wherever you feel pulled will be right for you.

I Ran Away From Home When I Was Just A Child

What does it mean?

For a very long time I didn't know. But the phrase kept playing in my head. It bothered me. I had often planned to run away but never did; I couldn't figure out the logistics (I was pretty sure my grandparents would send me straight back).

Years later, I dumped a guy. It was going nowhere. Then I felt like shit. So I did one of those online questionnaires (I was already in therapy) and chewed on it until it hit me. I was scared to be in a relationship because of a lot of the stuff that happened when I was a kid (what happened – none of your damn business – this is not that kind of book. This is not for spectators – get a life). I apologized to the guy, he kindly accepted and then 7/7 happened. I messaged everyone, but not him, it was too unthinkable that anything could have happened to him, my mind would not allow it (this is denial, I believe), I went to sleep and woke up with PTSD (post traumatic stress disorder).

That, I think was my first big step to waking up, coming alive, feeling my feelings and that was probably ten years ago (don't bother setting your watch, everybody's journey is different).

> I felt my fear. The fear I had been too scared to feel when I was a kid.
>
> Fear is big, right?

I just did a firewalk a few days ago and maybe that's why this is all happening now, because it was not scary at all. What they called fear I called excitement, energy, joy at having an adventure, at not being safe in a safe way (I may burn my feet, but I'm pretty sure I'm not going to die).

Fear, real fear? I can feel my eyes pricking right now because I can feel compassion for the little me, for being so scared that I was too scared to pee my pants. That's fear. When you are too scared to breathe, to cry, to move, too scared to even let your knees knock together (that's the fear of skateboarding down a ramp for the first time).

The human being is so incredible that it has an overload switch for fear, a built in redundancy that enables us to function at a level where we should die from the strength of our feelings.

I felt it when a tyre blew out on the motorway: Nothing… and then as the situation got easier, the recovery truck came, I got in my car and little by little the fear got worse, and then, as weird things happen when you're in flow, road works diverted me until I was driving past my childhood home for the first time in twenty years. I didn't stop shaking for a day.

That wasn't the main PTSD (it flares up occasionally) – the main PTSD was being afraid to sleep because of waking up with a panic attack, not being able to get in a car, not wanting to be in the house just wanting to walk everywhere, even late at night with the feeling "I am safer walking the streets at night than being in my own house." Barely functioning.

I can't be me if I can't feel my feelings. I can't be me if I can't get out of denial enough to feel my grief. I can't come back to myself unless I am prepared to be really fucking miserable, angry, resentful, misanthropic, bitter, twisted and hateful, oh and scared and sad (if such a small word can be used for grief).

When I woke up to my pain – the awakening, it was just after I had woken up to unconditional love, suddenly feeling that love that goes all the way around and comes right through us, through all of us. It's like understanding as a child that when the sun goes away it doesn't leave the planet, it's just on the other side. That all the things we thought we had to do to bring the sun back (because we weren't worthy) were nonsense – it was just shining on the other side of the planet for a while. And it makes sense because somewhere inside of us we know that if there were no sun, if there were no universal unconditional love, we would be a cold, dead planet.

Anyway, these are just words, which may not get in your head in a way you can understand, maybe you're not ready (I wasn't until I was) but if you don't trust me, trust your feelings.

So where was I? The awakening, right? What happened, how did it happen? I'm going to tell you, but do me a favour, take a breath and really listen to this bit, it's important.

Sorry, little preamble first: I research healing, massage and spa treatments around the world, it has to do with getting into my body, trying to enjoy the feeling of a massage instead of going somewhere else in my head, being naked, being touched, being loved, being cared for and not least paying for it – considering myself worthy of such treatment and such expense. Anyway my research and journey had finally lead me to a native American healing in Aji Spa in Chandler, Arizona with a wonderful woman named Belen Stoneman. It may be all down to her…

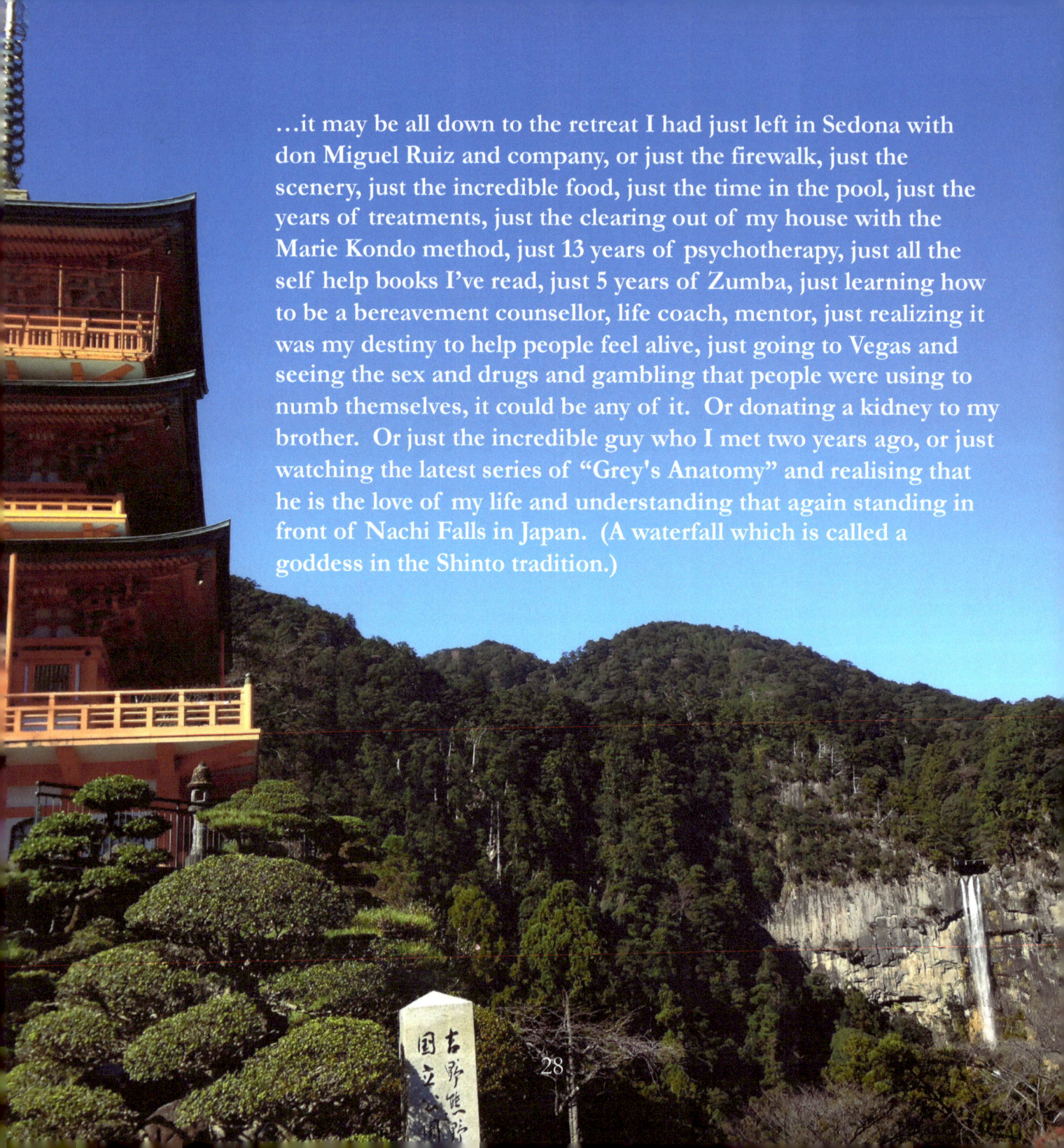

…it may be all down to the retreat I had just left in Sedona with don Miguel Ruiz and company, or just the firewalk, just the scenery, just the incredible food, just the time in the pool, just the years of treatments, just the clearing out of my house with the Marie Kondo method, just 13 years of psychotherapy, just all the self help books I've read, just 5 years of Zumba, just learning how to be a bereavement counsellor, life coach, mentor, just realizing it was my destiny to help people feel alive, just going to Vegas and seeing the sex and drugs and gambling that people were using to numb themselves, it could be any of it. Or donating a kidney to my brother. Or just the incredible guy who I met two years ago, or just watching the latest series of "Grey's Anatomy" and realising that he is the love of my life and understanding that again standing in front of Nachi Falls in Japan. (A waterfall which is called a goddess in the Shinto tradition.)

Okay, here we go. I cried like an injured animal. I felt my pain, feelings that are unnameable and unknowable even a few days later to me. I honoured myself, I honoured my pain. I felt my unconditional love for myself. I felt that I didn't have to be happy. I didn't have to make anyone else happy. I didn't even have to please myself. I was exhausted. Of trying so hard to be good, to smile, to be grateful, to be joyful, of pushing down my true self. Pushing down my knowing – the knowing at the centre of me (what some people might call the mind, body, spirit connection or my heart) in order to go against myself. Rationalising everything, looking for a silver lining, telling myself it didn't hurt, they didn't mean it, I just needed to get on with it, get with the program and serve others. Fuck others! What I felt at the bottom of it all was not happy, it was desperate, painful and lonely to cut myself off, to ignore my feelings, to pretend to be someone else, someone worthy of love and affection.

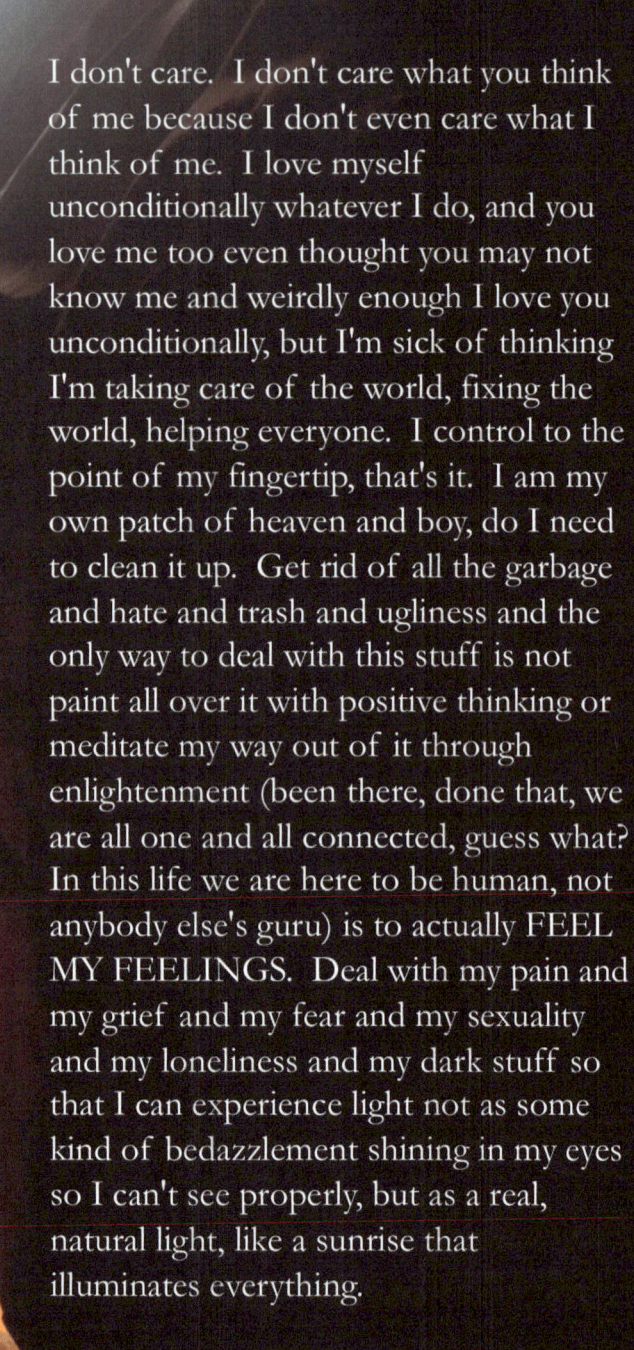

I don't care. I don't care what you think of me because I don't even care what I think of me. I love myself unconditionally whatever I do, and you love me too even thought you may not know me and weirdly enough I love you unconditionally, but I'm sick of thinking I'm taking care of the world, fixing the world, helping everyone. I control to the point of my fingertip, that's it. I am my own patch of heaven and boy, do I need to clean it up. Get rid of all the garbage and hate and trash and ugliness and the only way to deal with this stuff is not paint all over it with positive thinking or meditate my way out of it through enlightenment (been there, done that, we are all one and all connected, guess what? In this life we are here to be human, not anybody else's guru) is to actually FEEL MY FEELINGS. Deal with my pain and my grief and my fear and my sexuality and my loneliness and my dark stuff so that I can experience light not as some kind of bedazzlement shining in my eyes so I can't see properly, but as a real, natural light, like a sunrise that illuminates everything.

I saw the stars in Sedona and it changed my understanding of the universe, that beyond the stars there are just more stars, and galaxies, but I only saw this light because they shut down all the lights in the area to keep the sky dark.

You need to shut down the fake light to see the real light.

I did not see this sky in Vegas (but the sunrise was beautiful, I saw it from my suite, through my suite long windows that gave me a view from the mountains to the mini-Eiffel tower, from my king size bed. Jealous? I don't care.)

I felt the bear inside me, that roar of "leave me alone" so I can eat, sleep and shit when I want, so I can be grumpy or play or just roll around on the floor. And then I felt the eagle, that soaring feeling and the knowledge that I was free. The knowledge that the phrase "It Is Given" related not to money or wherewithal but to nothing less than free will. Not freedom, as none of us have perfect freedom, but what is given either by God or by our human nature, our free will, to choose for ourselves. The knowledge that I owed nothing to anyone and no one owed me anything (and if I did it was just a little bit of money and certainly not any part of my soul). I am free.

So that was that really, I woke up to myself. And all I could think of was the book "Rachel's Holiday" by Marian Keyes when the characters wake up to the knowledge that they are an alcoholic, drug addict, overeater, sex addict, whatever, and they ROAR!

Because all those feelings come up, all the ones pushed down and smothered in food, drugs, alcohol or even just plain old fashioned self-numbing that comes to us kids with sad stories (you can't teach that stuff) and everything that seemed important before seems a million miles away.

That job? I am more important.

The family and friends? I don't care what they think.

That "personal brand" – are you kidding me? Me, a brand? I'm like five minutes old because I just woke up after 44 fucking years of self numbing. And I cried and I roared and I sat on a porch of a ranch by myself (apart from a skunk – I kid you not) eating take out BBQ ribs, slept twelve hours, got through a familial style breakfast with everyone else staying at the ranch…

…decamped to Vegas with 12 hours in the car, alternating bawling my eyes out in the car to various songs, eating very good pecan pie in a diner, chicken salad in Sedona, spending a couple of hours hanging out with my animal teachers - the bear cubs in Bearizona, eating coconut cream pie (first time ever, I like it) before finally nearly being killed by a crazy driver and having a valet help me with my seventeen carrier bags into a suite at the Vdara (so nice) where I could finally go on retreat (well, my kind of retreat) knowing I didn't have to leave my room as they had 24/7 room service and no one knew me there.

And it came up… half an hour by the pool for breakfast before retiring to my room to throw a Snickers bar at the sofa… a little time in the Cosmopolitan Spa before crying and freaking out in the cold mist room and the steam room, before finally having a massage that helped ease my muscles and made me realise that you know, this journey to heal myself isn't half bad at times.

So yes, I may be suffering a little self-numbing hangover, a little "why did I do that to myself?!" but as I sit here I know I'm ready, that I've chucked out half of what I owned as the New Year struck, let go of some work, got my body in good shape, have a practice that works for me (when I don't overwork), know how to write and publish a book myself, have figured a lot of this shit out and this awakening happened because I was ready, ready to be for myself first, not to blame or make excuses for anything I've done to myself since I was 16. I was finally ready to be me, whether you like me or not, whether I like myself or not.

You see the thing about bears (as the guy at Bearizona explained) is that when they've been in captivity a long time they need to be taught how to be bears again, so until I figure out how to be me again I'm not worrying about a silly little thing like people's opinions.

Unconditional Love

Guess what? I love you. I love you unconditionally and guess what? You love me too, exactly that same way. And I've never even sent you a birthday card (unless of course you know me personally – but I often forget).

I've done enlightenment. Yup, done that meditation thing where I realise that we are connected, are the same atoms and felt it, really felt it, so I know that when things get scary this human thing is just a game. But still. I believed that we are not here to be just focused on the spiritual, I mean after all we have these beautiful bodies, these minds (and we have sex! And massage. And food!) so I also believed this, which I love - "We are not human beings on a spiritual journey, we are spiritual beings on a human journey." So I got that I wasn't here to be a Buddhist nun or just sit in meditation, I am here to be human and have a great old time, but I always prayed "Dear Lord, make me a better person" every night.

How could I be a better me?

I had a relationship which unravelled much of what I thought
was me and so I was coming to a retreat in Sedona, a
gathering with don Miguel Ruiz and friends with an
understanding that much of what I felt was me
was just emotional poison, and a desire to be
happier, freer, more successful, I guess
more powerful.
To see if I had the strength and wisdom to
run retreats, to learn and figure some stuff out.
What did I want to get out of the retreat?
Well, if I knew that
I probably wouldn't have had to do it.

So on the first night
don Miguel Ruiz talks about
unconditional love. How we all feel it for
each other, for ourselves, but we have a
relationship with our beloved and we say this:
"Darling, I love you so much, if you would
just do what I tell you we could have such a happy life."
And we laughed, I laughed, thinking "Yes, this is me,
but what else is there? How do I live another way?"

So I went to bed, thinking, I am just not getting this.

…and I saw the stars and more stars and more stars and galaxies and I felt it. I felt unconditional love and I understood and started to write my apology to my beloved.

I will always love him, even if he meets and marries someone else. Just like I would love my nieces and nephews even if they committed the most terrible crime and were in prison.

The problem is never the lack of love.

I love my father. And I finally forgive myself for loving my father when he really wasn't very good at being a father. But I love him anyway. And I forgive him too. I see the pain in him was really him trying to be good, to go against himself and then go the other way because it wasn't in him. His failings were his failings, not my fault.

And I know that he loved me unconditionally too, which is rather nice to know after all the years of torturing myself over whether he loved me (or even remembered which one I was) or not.

When we hold a baby we feel that incredible love that goes all the way around and through the planet. That's our big and wonderful mystery and influences all our other mysteries and we would do anything for that love, we would die, we would kill, but what we do is we domesticate.

I remember when my very small niece, just a couple of years old, decided to run away and hide as a game in a department store at Christmas. I think my heart stopped until I saw her again. I screamed at her, she cried and I told her off "Don't ever do that again!"

All our rules, all our beliefs, we build from the people saying they want to protect us, like Rapunzel in a tower. It's no life.

Life is adventure and excitement, it's unsafe and wonderful and magical and we get hurt if we live exciting lives but we hurt ourselves if we live too safe.

"Playing it safe is just about the most dangerous thing a woman like you can do." Moonstruck

So I felt it. Unconditional love for everyone, and for myself. And I think that was a big step in letting myself heal, accepting and loving myself as I truly am (or as I think I am!) and woe betide anyone who comes up and judges me or looks me up and down or says something mean right now. I love you unconditionally but I don't control you, I control me and I tell you I have just started letting me be me after trying to be "good" and "happy" and "a better person" so I will tell you to fuck right off if you try and put me back in my cage.

I'm FREEE!!!!

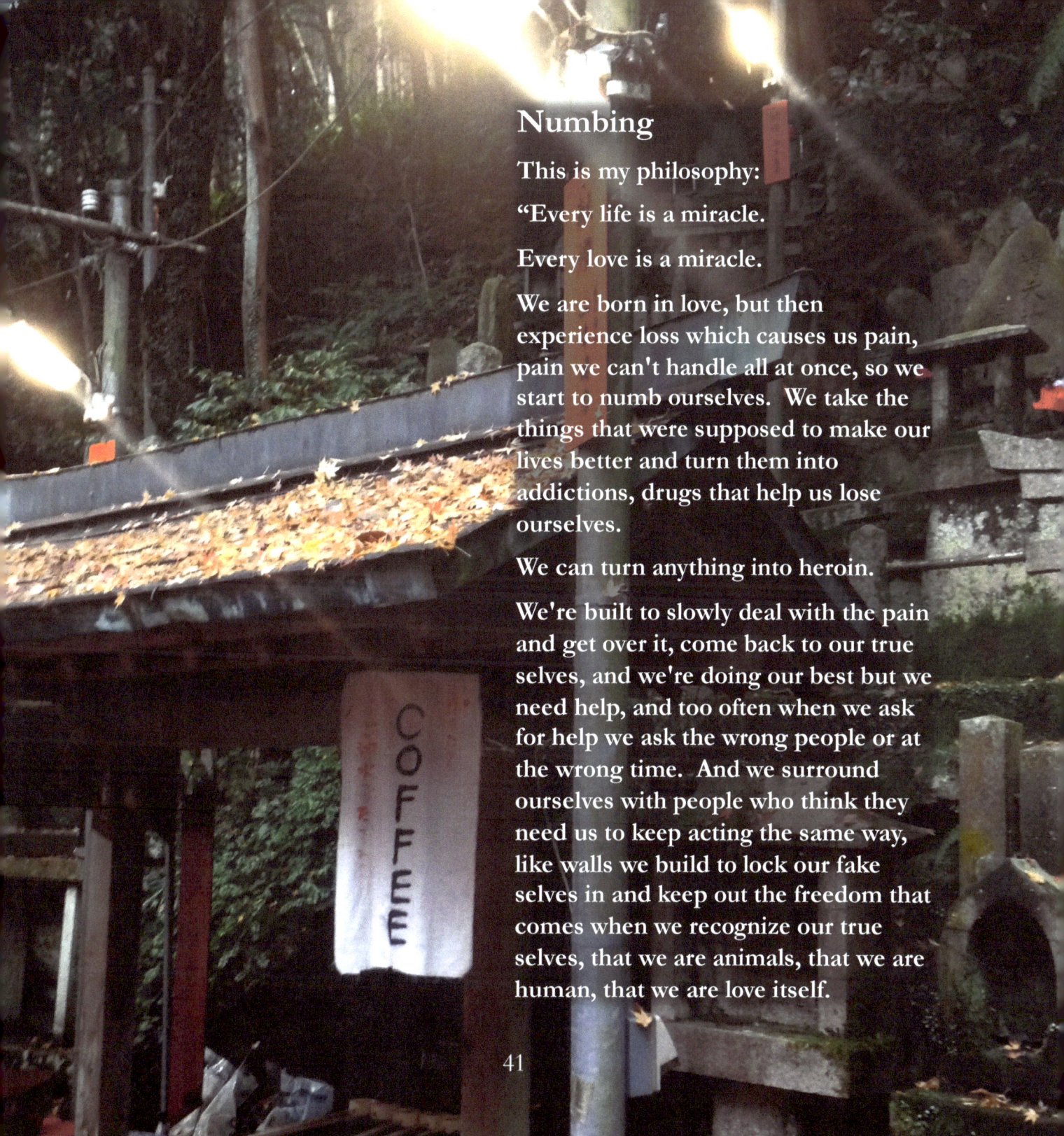

Numbing

This is my philosophy:

"Every life is a miracle.

Every love is a miracle.

We are born in love, but then experience loss which causes us pain, pain we can't handle all at once, so we start to numb ourselves. We take the things that were supposed to make our lives better and turn them into addictions, drugs that help us lose ourselves.

We can turn anything into heroin.

We're built to slowly deal with the pain and get over it, come back to our true selves, and we're doing our best but we need help, and too often when we ask for help we ask the wrong people or at the wrong time. And we surround ourselves with people who think they need us to keep acting the same way, like walls we build to lock our fake selves in and keep out the freedom that comes when we recognize our true selves, that we are animals, that we are human, that we are love itself.

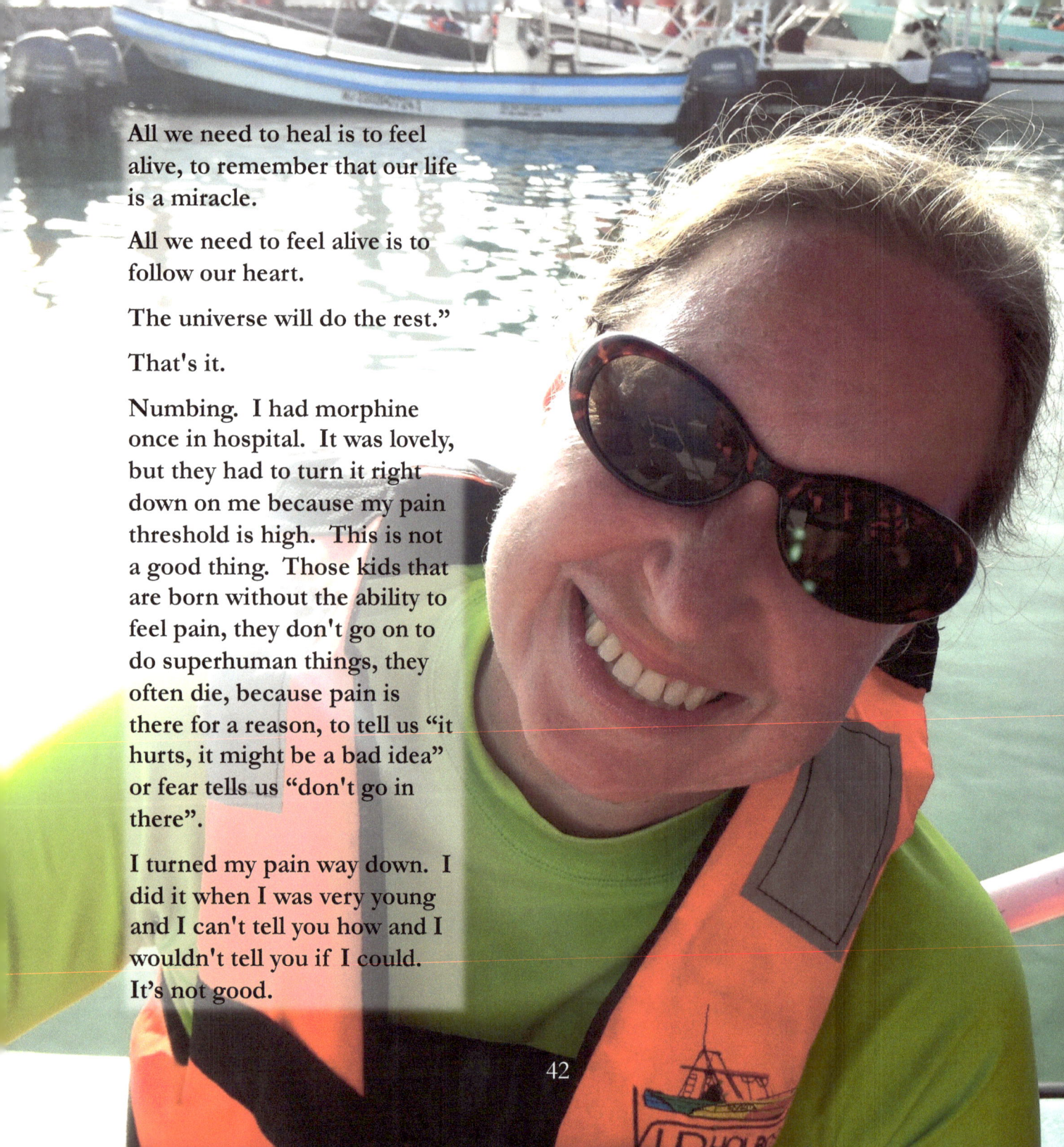

All we need to heal is to feel alive, to remember that our life is a miracle.

All we need to feel alive is to follow our heart.

The universe will do the rest."

That's it.

Numbing. I had morphine once in hospital. It was lovely, but they had to turn it right down on me because my pain threshold is high. This is not a good thing. Those kids that are born without the ability to feel pain, they don't go on to do superhuman things, they often die, because pain is there for a reason, to tell us "it hurts, it might be a bad idea" or fear tells us "don't go in there".

I turned my pain way down. I did it when I was very young and I can't tell you how and I wouldn't tell you if I could. It's not good.

Letting Go of My Pride

My first Zumba class was piss poor. I did my best, I was practising religiously. It was still a terrible mess. It doesn't hurt my pride to tell you because I think I'm pretty good now.

At the retreat in Sedona we did a blessing way (inspired by traditional native American rituals). They said, "In order to move forward to the next step in your life there is something holding you back, something you need to let go of." I figured it was pride, ego, thinking I was better than everyone else. We picked up a stone to symbolise the thing we needed to let go of. We walked into the centre of the circle and dropped it. It took me ages. We tied red string around our wrists, to remind us to let go of that thing that was holding us back.

It was in the native American healing with Belen that I let go. Let go and felt everything I had been pushing down. In that moment my ego was destroyed. In that moment there was no pride, the idea that I was better than anyone else, that it mattered what other people thought of me was just ridiculous. Me was the person I had been pushing down because I thought I was worse than everyone else, because I thought I didn't deserve to be. I had been hiding, pretending to be someone else for so long that I thought I was the character I was playing. Coming back to myself was the awakening. I tore off the red string.

I am blessed to have studied Zumba for so long, to have worked on the understanding of ego, to believe we are all equal, to know we are all doing our best, to be able to hear "I don't like that new song" or "You're the best teacher ever" and know it is more about them than me. I don't need to defend myself or judge others. I just am, am doing my best today (I think it's pretty damn good - but I could be wrong).

I am doing my best to be without pride in my relationship. It still hurts when he chooses not be with me, not to call, not to text, but I can stop the self-talk that blames me, my actions or who I am, the track that says I am worthless. It still tears me apart not to be with him but I don't blame him and I don't blame me.

I write books. I think I'm a pretty good writer, but I am who I am. I can see a five star review, or a one star review and it doesn't get me. I have to do my best to let go of pride when I write, how else could I tell the truth? I have to do my best to let go of pride when I instruct, how else could I tell the truth? I have to do my best to let go of pride when I speak, how else could I tell the truth?

I serve the student, I serve the reader, I serve the listener.

But then I tried to be an author. A bestselling author, no less.

Turns out my first attempt at coming out of hiding as a writer was piss poor. The ego walloped back in. Book sales, support, likes, blessings, it all became a curse because it fed my ego, my pride my "I'm better, I'm so special."

When I woke up again I looked around and saw I'd started judging everyone again. Little things, what someone was wearing, feeling superior because I had more Facebook Friends (can you be more superficial than that?)

And in judging others, once again I was judging myself, comparing myself. There is no way to judge others without judging ourselves, it cuts both ways.

But there is no way forward without occasionally slipping and falling. Pride is such a difficult drug to avoid. I like Iggy Pop's method of rehab. He says once you get clean for three days if you put something bad in your system you feel it immediately and say "Hey, I was feeling so good, what happened?" Then at least you know you slipped up.

Knowing Not Thinking (Road Closed)

So I know things. Feelings. If I go for a wander and follow my feet or my heart I get in flow and miracles happen, coincidences, meetings, signs. Like my body knowing it could walk over fire. Like knowing even if there is a sign saying "Footpath Closed" they haven't started the work. Or another time my body knowing it shouldn't go the usual way, ignoring it and finding out that road *was* closed.

In the past it has freaked me out.

Or the first few letters of the first Scrabble game of the year - Vegas. Or seeing ghosts. That scared me, because I never wanted to believe in ghosts. I was driving late at night, so maybe it was my brain playing tricks, trying to stop me falling asleep, but I never took that road again at night.

I see things, in my dreams, and sometimes during massages or healings.

Here's how I make sense of it - with the ghosts I didn't die or run off the road so that's a good thing. I'm happy to leave the rest a mystery.

As for the visions, I may or may not understand them. They can be completely literal, i.e. I see a bird in my vision and later I see a bird, I feel bears and then I go to Bearizona, I see a wedding dress – it does not mean a wedding – it could mean a lively discussion about marriage or that I try on wedding dresses with a friend. If I see body bags, I remind everyone to drive safe.

How do I explain it? I can't, but I have theories and my biggest one is this; we are all connected and where we are connected is not physical or even spiritual or mental but in the mind, body, spirit connection, so the more we get in flow, into bliss if you like, the more we follow our hearts the more intuitive we become. Our physical senses also hone, that awareness, so we notice more "coincidences".

I was talking to my native American healer about knowing, "What do you do." I asked. "Well" she said "what do you do?" Without thinking it popped out 'I push it down".

I pushed down the sense of knowing along with my other feelings because it was too painful to know and not follow my heart.

I pushed down the knowing that I loved and missed my beloved so much, that we should be together, because everyone told me it was crazy, because I was scared to get hurt again, because I thought I should play it safe, but it was my knowing and his that brought us together.

There are so many things we know, especially about our lovers and our friends and family, and yet we push them down because we're afraid.

What I learned from the fire walk is that rational thinking doesn't always work, trusting instinctive knowing is often wisest.

The Love Of My Life

I met the love of my life on a beach nearly two years ago. I listened to my heart and it called me to Clearwater Beach, beneath the full moon. The year before I witnessed something magical on the beach, I still don't know what it was, it's still a mystery, or maybe he was the answer?

I left the hotel before sunrise, walked across the street and saw him in the spot where the water turns gold when the first ray of sun hits the moon. We talked, swam, I turned my head and thought "He's alright". His hand brushed mine and I felt a shock.

I knew in my heart this was where I had been heading my whole life, everything made sense. I met that magical person; "my soul's counterpart in another human being", the romantic connection I just didn't believe in. Until I did. And we knew we were so lucky to have found each other.

But the doubt set in. All the beliefs we had been taught, all the judgment, all the fear and sometimes, when we let it, it was magic and other times it was clunky and weird. And we were tired, what with all that time difference and jetlag and worrying about making enough money so that what if we had to live in a country where one of us couldn't work because of the visa situation…

Love hurts. So they tell you.

I want to tell you right now (and write it so I never, ever, ever, ever forget again). Love is easy, it's the easiest, most fluid, beautiful thing in the world. Until you try to control the other person. Until you try to be someone else because you worry that you're not good enough. Until you get so confused and in pain that you have to go away and numb the pain with work or perfectionism or alcohol or five star spas or you start screaming at the other person because you can't see that what they are "doing to you" is what you are doing to yourself.

Love is free.

Love is freeing.

Love is accepting the other person just as they are (that judgment is just me worrying what I think and what everyone else will think about them – let it go).

Love is opening up your heart and feeling free to be yourself with the other person who sees you and knows you and loves you openly when you forgot how to love yourself. And then you tell yourself that you can't be that person (when that person is only your real self that you rejected long ago).

Anything is possible.

Love is the greatest adventure, the greatest escape. It is not safe. You may get hurt. But truly what hurts so much more is all that judgment.

All the fricking rules.

You have to have sex on the third date… once a week… once a month.

You have to move in after six months, or a year, or not until you're married.

You have to get married.

You have to live together. You have to make enough money before you can live together. What about health benefits? What if you get pregnant?

You have to be exclusive, or you have to be open-minded. You have to have that conversation. You have to talk about your exes or never talk about your exes.

He has to call you, you can't call him. You have to stop texting so he'll call you.

You have to see each other at least once a week.

You have to meet his parents.

You don't want to invest your time in a relationship that's going nowhere.

…or someone who might not want what you want in five years time.

You have to buy a card and chocolates and flowers on Valentine's Day…

On the retreat I met so many people who had followed their heart and met someone, they knew as soon as they saw each other, or touched a hand, or saw the way someone walked. It's real love people, real as the love of the girl next door who you grew up with or the guy you met and talked to for eight months on an internet dating website. Some people just know.

And some people might be having that love all the time, they just didn't experience it that way.

I wish I had not gone against myself, against my knowing, against my love because I was so scared of getting hurt, listened to so many judgments and beliefs and judged myself so much. I want to say it's all wonderful because it's brought me here, to a place where I know I was meant to be, but I still miss the love of my life.

Native Healing

So what is native healing? Well there are two meanings, one is the native American healing that I received at Aji Spa in Chandler, Arizona from Belen Stoneman. More about that in a mo. The other is the path I have been on for a very long time, being drawn to massages and treatments. It really started in Moroccco in a hammam, just a change of pace on a surfing holiday, with a traditional scrubbing and massage and a falling away, not just of the dead skin on my body but layers of belief. My skin was not my skin, those flakey patches, that dry skin, those spotty bits you know, my "problem skin"...

Gone.

No chemicals, lotions or tablets, just a scrubbing glove that cost a couple of pennies, some black soap, a hot bath and a woman not afraid to scrub away everything she knew was dead on my body. And then the most incredible massage. Ancient healing. And understanding, I wished I was wearing a full Arabic dress, because my clean, clean skin was getting covered in dirty old dust. I thought "we are so dirty compared to them – they do this once a month and I've never done it in my life." The next day I couldn't surf, I just had to be alone, walk among the dunes by myself, grieve for a loss I knew was coming (and when that loss came I couldn't stop crying – who knows what would have happened if I hadn't been able to grieve for at least a part of it beforehand).

>We use the words mind, body and spirit as if we could separate
>them, maybe because we've separated ourselves from
>the land, the water, the sky and fire too,
>but we need all of these for life.

Back to the native American healing at Aji. It's called Thoachta or Healing.

I'm an explorer and a writer and sometimes it feels my experience is not complete until I've shared it with the world. (I want to share so much right now because I've woken up and am experiencing a new dream of life, which at times feels overwhelming).

But sometimes I over-share. Sometimes when I see a delicious meal I take a photo and think of how to describe it, am trying to give it to everyone before I give it to myself.

When I sat with Belen I was aware of this, so I promised myself to close the door, allow the sacred to happen for me and me alone, experience the healing for me and not for some potential reader. But, as I said in the Introduction, I realise the reader I was writing for was me, as if I was carrying my true self within me, protected, confined. So because I was no longer transcribing for that secret self she had to come into the room.

I talked. I felt my pain, in my words, my spirit, wracking through my body. I felt my grief. We took a moment. I laid down and then Belen started to work on my body. I felt bored. I felt myself switching off, so I told myself to be present, feel my feelings, be curious, allow the healing.

I heard myself say I don't have to be happy, I don't have to keep trying to make myself happy. These are just words. The words I felt were lonely, desperate and in pain, the pain of the belief that being sad was bad, of putting away my feelings, hiding them from others, from myself and "faking it till I make it", of not being good enough for myself. In that moment I made the decision at last not to be positive or grateful or happy or content or anything, I made the decision to just be me. To just sit and observe myself, or a tree, without judgement, without conditions, to let go of the beliefs I had built up about myself, who I was, what I could be, where I could go, how I could live, everything, who were my friends, my lovers, how I could be free, and just be free. Finally.

And it hurt so bad. I was destroyed, or rather my ego, that little fake person I had built and carried with me (that thought it was carrying me). She was pretty cool, she was so, so concerned with others. I am concerned with me.

The first couple of days I wondered if I would ever care about anyone else again. My care was all for me. I tried not to offend anyone, but I had to take care of myself, because I had neglected myself.

And then slowly it happened, I hung out by the pool and I played, I sat with the bears in Bearizona and I smiled and exchanged a few words with strangers about how cool the bears were. Slowly I filled up my own tank, put my own oxygen mask on and I could feel the love, unconditional love starting to spill over to the other people in my life (not too much now, not all at once, don't be getting in that bad habit again).

I am playing in my own dream now.

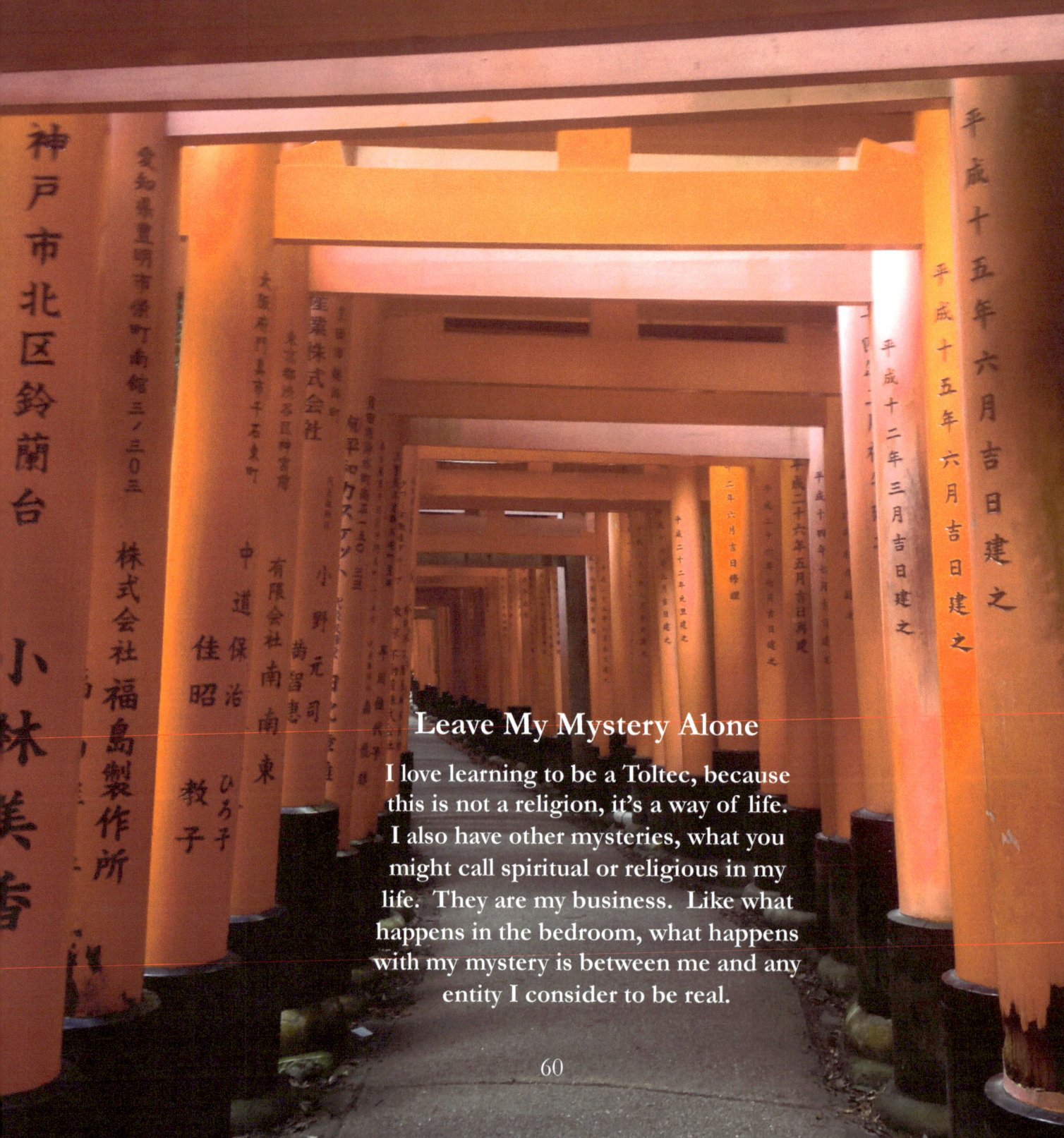

Leave My Mystery Alone

I love learning to be a Toltec, because this is not a religion, it's a way of life. I also have other mysteries, what you might call spiritual or religious in my life. They are my business. Like what happens in the bedroom, what happens with my mystery is between me and any entity I consider to be real.

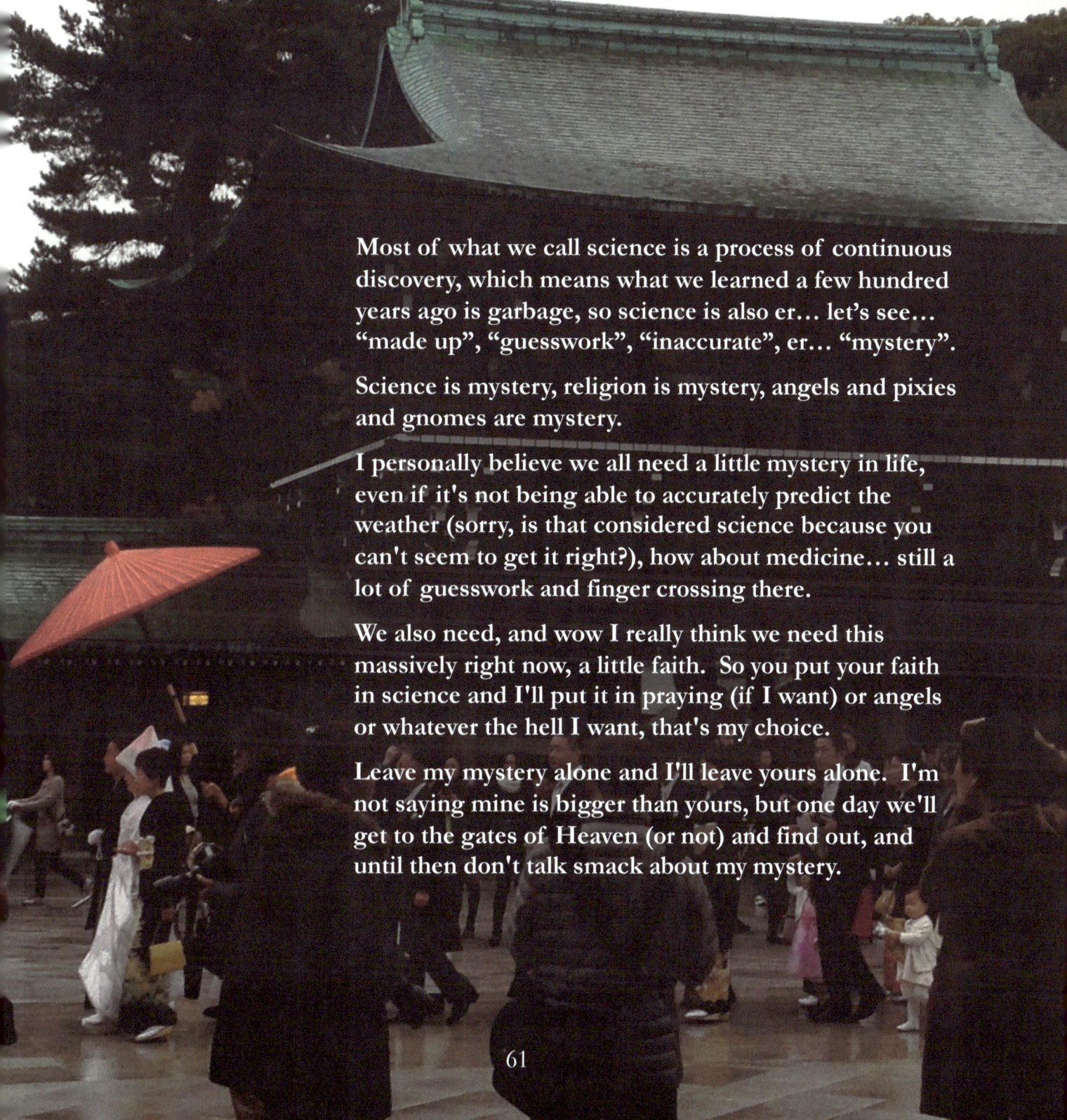

Most of what we call science is a process of continuous discovery, which means what we learned a few hundred years ago is garbage, so science is also er… let's see… "made up", "guesswork", "inaccurate", er… "mystery".

Science is mystery, religion is mystery, angels and pixies and gnomes are mystery.

I personally believe we all need a little mystery in life, even if it's not being able to accurately predict the weather (sorry, is that considered science because you can't seem to get it right?), how about medicine… still a lot of guesswork and finger crossing there.

We also need, and wow I really think we need this massively right now, a little faith. So you put your faith in science and I'll put it in praying (if I want) or angels or whatever the hell I want, that's my choice.

Leave my mystery alone and I'll leave yours alone. I'm not saying mine is bigger than yours, but one day we'll get to the gates of Heaven (or not) and find out, and until then don't talk smack about my mystery.

You think you have the same mystery as me? I do not care. You think because I am Anglo, white, female, heterosexual (so far) and, possibly, Christian that you can come here and tell me what my mystery should be? Hell no. You think you can judge me because I do or do not pray, wear a crucifix, believe in sex before marriage, believe in purgatory or original sin or whatever. No, leave it alone.

You want me to listen to what you have to say about mystery? Go and live in Calcutta and wash lepers' feet for forty years and then you can have five minutes of my time. If you use that time to talk about the evil of condoms it cuts down to two minutes.

I respect many people and their opinions, but don't ever try and tell me what to believe when it comes to the unseen. That's my business.

If I am indeed a shaman – maybe I am, maybe I'm not – one definition is someone who connects to the unseen, whether that is love, God, energy, knowing the unknowable... So if I am a shaman then the unseen is exactly my business – and I treat it with great honour and care, so don't fuck with it.

Leave My Money Alone

I've said it a lot before and yet I'm still learning it – we have sooooo much on money and sex, it's like the two big topics and what sells media, right? What happens in someone's bedroom between consenting, respectful adults – nobody's business but theirs. I really, really don't care. And I really, really don't want to know.

Somebody's money? Their business. My money? My business. I am helped in this a little because in England we think it's rude to talk about money i.e. what do you earn, but then we're even more judgmental about anything financial that hints at class (e.g. sections on a plane – you put the word class in there and it's a red rag to us).

I have some very lovely friends and family who care about me and so try to protect me by telling me that I spend too much on what I want, or that I don't make enough money.

Excerpt from today's conversation:

Me: "It's my money."

Loved One: "But…"

Me: "It's my money."

Loved One: "But…"

Me: "It's my money."

Loved One: "But you need to make more money and sort yourself out financially…"

Me: "I'm rich, I've just come back from Vegas where I stayed in 5 star hotels, I've just done the most incredible retreat and had fantastic massages, I've done nearly everything I want to do in life and worse case scenario I can sell my house and go live somewhere cheap."

You see this is the bollocks… the phrase "financial freedom". It's been whored out to the people who want you to be afraid, very afraid of money so this is what they tell you…

Get a good job where someone else will tell you what to do, don't worry if you hate it or get paid tuppence or it's a little immoral or makes you hate yourself because that's what everyone else does, it's called paying your dues, (one day you'll get to turn around and

see your juniors do it and
then you can abuse them), then
start a pension fund, where the money
you put in will be held in trust for you so you
can relax and have a great time when you can feel
nothing but the pain of being old (in trust means it will be
given to corporations and governments in shares and bonds so that
effectively you are shoring up the big amoral organizations of the world),
okay, then you need to get on the property ladder so you can pay an exorbitant
mortgage to the banks (who is winning this game so far, can you see?), then if
you have any money left we'd like to offer you broadband and a TV package, still
got money left, let's sell you a fancy car that we can advertise to you on the TV
you paid for. But you need this stuff, you earned it, right? Oh and then you need
to insure it all so you can have "financial freedom" in case anything goes wrong.

Here is what I call financial freedom… Ready…

Knowing that you are more important than money.

It breaks my heart that there are places all over the world where people have to consider the cost of a life. Life saving medical treatment, mosquito nets… in some countries at some times it is pennies, other times to save your child's life you may have to go thousands and thousands of pounds into debt.

How much is your life worth?

Not how much are YOU worth? Because I think it's demeaning to think like that at all. (There are no prizes for dying with a fat bank account and a big house.) I kind of know how much would be left if I died and my house was sold and debts paid off and I'm satisfied that no one would have to suffer for my financial freedom.

I have gone against myself for money. Time and time again. Got out of bed and worked when I had flu, chest infections, stomach bugs, back pain, torn muscles. Gone against myself by working for people who I knew were immoral and unethical (and possibly illegal) and excused myself on the grounds that I was only doing the creative stuff, I wasn't selling that shit (but I was part of the sales process).

I have eaten cheap, bad food not because I didn't have the money but because I treated my body as though it were expendable and money as precious.

I have cheapskated myself out of amazing trips and wonderful things. I have abused myself and put money first.

I have listened to potential clients drone on, too afraid to say goodbye in case they would buy at some point, I have undercharged, I have worked for free in the hope I would get some paid work, I have pitied people and charged them so little it demeans us both.

And I guess that makes me some kind of whore, because I did not work with love, I just did it for the money.

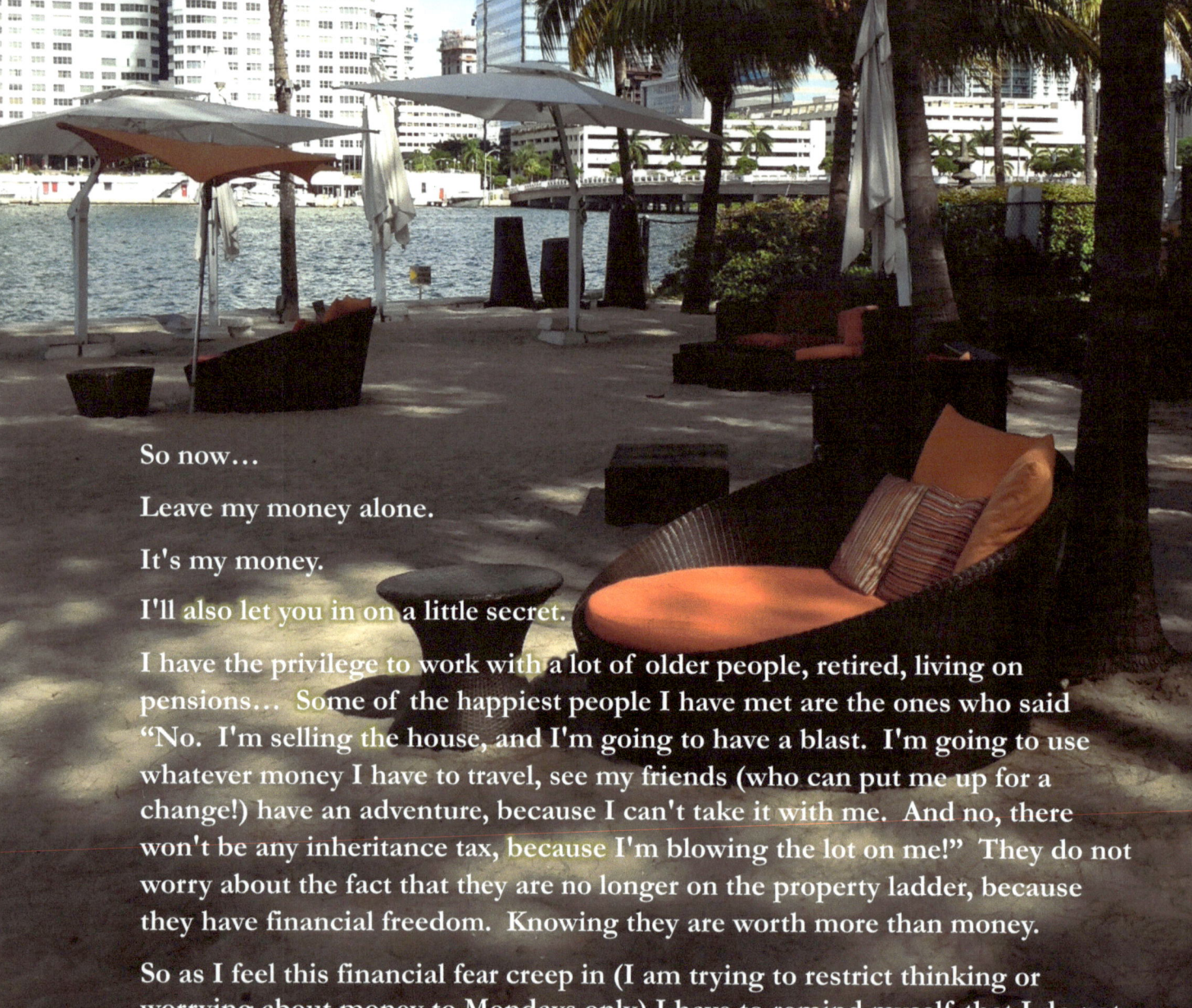

So now…

Leave my money alone.

It's my money.

I'll also let you in on a little secret.

I have the privilege to work with a lot of older people, retired, living on pensions… Some of the happiest people I have met are the ones who said "No. I'm selling the house, and I'm going to have a blast. I'm going to use whatever money I have to travel, see my friends (who can put me up for a change!) have an adventure, because I can't take it with me. And no, there won't be any inheritance tax, because I'm blowing the lot on me!" They do not worry about the fact that they are no longer on the property ladder, because they have financial freedom. Knowing they are worth more than money.

So as I feel this financial fear creep in (I am trying to restrict thinking or worrying about money to Mondays only) I have to remind myself that I do not want to be a whore for money in any shape or form.

If I cannot do this work (write, dance, teach, speak) with love, do I have the guts to not do it at all?

Leave My Body Alone

Seriously when it did become okay for people to care so much about everyone else's bodies?

My body. Not your body.

None. Of. Your. Damn. Business.

I don't have the same passion for this because I look hot right now. One of the things I have loved over the past few days of this awakening is taking the time to get naked in front of the mirror and dance it up, admire myself, think shit, I AM GORGEOUS. Not stand around being apologetic… "Oh yes, well I'm okay…"

No, please, I'm pretty much broke and have been pushing my feelings down for years and right now would love a chocolate brownie, but… why shouldn't I swagger about how good I look?

I love seeing a baby with a mirror, they dance around, they get naked, they look at everything (and I mean EVERYTHING!) And then they get taught it's inappropriate. Stop taking all your clothes off in public, stop touching yourself, stop admiring yourself, stop telling yourself you are beautiful because you are too fat, too thin, too white, too dark, too blonde, too curly, too tall, too short.

Fuck that shit.

I would love to shred every magazine that ever published an unflattering, judgmental photo of anyone and use that as confetti in a parade to how gorgeous and wonderful and magical and perfect we are.

(By the way the pics are from the Bikini Challenge on the Lorraine show in the UK. The closest we have to Oprah I guess. Yes, live national TV in a bikini.)

I know I can't run around with no clothes on (I actually spent this afternoon trying to keep a floaty skirt down in high winds when I was wearing a nude colour thong so I really don't want to even flash the world)… but I can sunbathe in the park in my bikini or bra if I came unprepared… I can show off a lovely back in a low cut top… and my cleavage, well… it would be a crime against nature not to let that out every so often.

I love me, I love my body and I love your body too (don't send me photos, I beg you). We can love each other, not judge each other, not be all like, "Well she's put on a few pounds" or "I don't like the colour of her hair" or "How's she gonna get a boyfriend when she's so tall?" Talk about something else, maybe how much you love yourself?

Does that leave you a lot of time? Write a book about how much you love yourself.

LEAVE MY BODY ALONE.

I Don't Have To Like Myself

When I woke up to unconditional love it gave me the wonderful freedom to not like myself… when the spoiled brat in me flares up… when I get angry… when I offend someone or am selfish. I can just observe. I don't have to fix myself. I don't have to be nice to everyone I meet, or pretend to like them (some people give me the heebie jeebies). I can stand up for myself and be a pain in the ass and not like the way it makes me feel so uncomfortable or that someone is going to think I'm pretentious or up myself or that I just love myself so much.

Because I do.

Let me clarify, I don't want to be a monster. And I am still finding my feet. I was talking to a waitress and I was trying to be simpler (I have this habit of chatting so much to everyone and I don't want to do it, but it's so hard to break, so I was even trying to answer "yes, no, maybe". I could not do it. The other night I was trying to leave the building and I was just going to say 'Goodnight" to the security guard. I couldn't help adding "have a great evening." Stop. It. I do not have to be everyone's best friend!) Anyway so the waitress was leaving and (I also see how badly some people treat staff, as if just because someone is providing a service you can treat them like shit – and I do not buy that AT ALL) so I said to the waitress; "Oh I'm so sorry I forgot to say Thank You." And she says "Don't worry sweetie, I get the vibe."

Phew!

I don't think of myself as a people pleaser, but I don't want to be a people hurter. I don't care if someone thinks I'm an asshole, but I do care if they feel bad. But the truth is they might take it personally anyway. What am I gonna do, date someone so that they don't feel bad? Okay so I have gone on dates for that reason, I have kept friends way overlong for that reason, I have kept clients…

Oh.

They say writing is cathartic.

Being a good person (or my definition of good) can be exhausting.

I don't have to like myself right now, because I need to be loved so much more. I need that unconditional love so I can eat, sleep, ignore phone messages, walk away when a client wants to talk to me for 3 (unpaid) hours about my classes. When some fucker wants to sell me something.

As I said to the bell desk woman when she rang to check whether I had received my laundry. "I have my do not disturb on, I am trying to sleep and you have had a guy come up and this is the second time you've called me, I know you are trying to be good but PLEASE, Leave Me Alone."

I Am An Eagle

Just before I went to Sedona I spent the night in Winslow, Arizona (it's such a fine place to be). I didn't even know it was a real place. I loved it. I took it easy.

In the morning I saw a place on the map next door called Toltec Divide (I was about to study with Toltecs/become a Toltec... whatever). Another reminder that my heart was calling me in the right direction.

I am an eagle. I saw it in a meditation on money some years ago, when I was stressing about paying the mortgage but still brave enough to pay a therapist to help me through. I fly. I didn't really know what it meant, but it has helped me many times when I don't fit in with the crowd.

I fly alone.

I don't fly like a goose. They switch so that one flies at the front and then they all get a rest. If I try to fly with geese I just fly at the front until I get pissed and exhausted at them all getting a free ride. It's just the way it is.

Eagles mate for life.

But even an eagle needs rest.

They were the most successful group ever because they were formed as a super group – each one a master. Their name came about during a peyote fuelled vision quest in the desert. They became The Eagles.

They nearly killed each other when they toured through drink and drugs and because they were all leaders. (Eagles usually fly alone for this reason.)

They had to split up to stop tearing each other apart.

And then they came back together years later, sober and made even more music history.

Their drummer, one of the craziest men in rock n'roll, said, in retrospect, now sober, that your life seems like a random chaotic madness as you live it, then as you look back it makes perfect sense. I can see a little of that now.

As I drove through Arizona I heard a wisdom in the words of The Eagles songs that I had never really appreciated, from the cheap talk and wine in the Best of My Love to laying with you in the desert tonight, with a billion stars all around. And, of course, there is the magic of Standing on the Corner in Winslow, Arizona where a little piece of Route 66 still lives. "We may lose or we may win but we will never be here again."

N.B. Turtles, although ridiculously cute, hate all other animals equally, even other turtles. It's a wonder they manage to mate.

Why I Hate Being Grateful

A couple of days ago (before awakening – BA) I was typing on Instagram #feelgratitude_feeljoy.

Now? I don't want to tell myself how to feel, let alone anyone else. The reason I wrote it?

Brené Brown says we resist joy because we're scared of loss, so by feeling grateful we can feel joyful. It totally works. You can also keep a diary by your bed and write down everything that you're grateful for each day (which will bite you in the ass when you have broken up with your boyfriend and read about all the blissful times you shared together).

In "Out of Africa" Karen Blixen is asked, "How can you stand losing everything?" She remembers how good it all was and then, when she thinks she can't stand it any more, she goes one second longer. "And then I know I can stand anything."

When I was a kid I couldn't say "Thank you". It stuck in my throat, maybe things would be taken back if they realized how much they were giving me (little old me)? I remember a present all my brothers and sisters made for me, my breath caught in my throat I was so overwhelmed. I took it to school and showed everyone. It was a cereal box with pictures they had stuck on for me. (I still think it was pretty cool.)

There's a name for this feeling, it's called "worthlessness". Yes, for some people feeling gratitude in order to feel joy may be helpful, may work, but for me it sucks and it's no way to feel good about myself.

I once found my childhood diaries in which I'd written about the wonderful things I had bought at the jumble sale, how truly lucky I was. I burned them, it was too painful, because I remember how much I hate wearing second hand clothes. I don't need any trick to remember the incredible joy I felt the first time my mother bought me my first brand new outfit. Thank you mum, I love you.

It's wonderful to be able to say "Thank you" and even more wonderful for me to be able to say "I love you", without being afraid that it will ruin the magic, that it will bring everything to a grinding halt, that it might not be said back to me. I can say "I love you, I love you , I love you"
      and it means nothing and everything
      because I know now that love goes all
      around us… and the stuff? The stuff is
          all around us too, we don't need to wipe
            the feet of anyone who gives us
            money, opportunities or
            attention — we are
              worthy of it all
              just by being.

I am sincere when I say "thank you". What I don't feel anymore is the obsequious "thank you for noticing me" gratitude that's just nasty. It's the cowering dog that has been abused looking for love in a scrap of food.

Everyone on this planet deserves the basics; clean water, healthcare, nutrition, public transportation, education or at least access to books (hell, we can't all afford Kindles even in the "developed" world). And we shouldn't have to abase ourselves for the luxuries. I am a wild young bohemian, if I have some cash I can spend it on fuel for the fire or a wild night out.

A word is just a symbol, it's only meaning is what we agree on, so these few words; gratitude, thankfulness, appreciation can mean a world of emotions …and the word grateful still sticks in my throat as the word of a little girl who doesn't believe she deserves anything – so right now it's out of my vocabulary.

Self-Imposed Slavery

I started reading "Walden", which is about two hundred years old and I was shocked that he a slave than the poor enslaved man on a plantation, all for the money to build a house and

He is often quoted as saying "most men live lives of quiet desperation"… often in business

The closest I have come in a recent book is "The Four Hour Work Week" which has a lot to make money remotely", "travel", "then go help people". I thought it was "help people" simpler… "follow your heart and you will become free", "money comes along".

It's ancient wisdom - it's all there in "The Four Agreements", "The Mastery of Love", "The

So it breaks my heart that I can read other books that are two hundred or just a few years old

was talking about everything I'm thinking and how "civilized man makes himself more of live at the standard of his neighbours". (Or words to that effect).

success books. Are they not missing the point? The point is to be free.

of good stuff in it, but still didn't quite work for me. Tim Ferriss' process is "find a way "make money doing that", then "travel", which I think is more fun. But it's so much

Fifth Agreement". Or go on retreat with the Ruiz family. They're lovely.

and see how much we are still enslaving ourselves.

I think about my beautiful, marvelous, wonderful friend (okay, lover) who I "lost" because he left a great career and many top qualifications behind to go and explore South America.

How I laughed when I finally arrived in Mexico years later, as I looked up at the adobe ceiling of my lovely hotel and thought of how I told him I would come and share his tent. I would have lasted five minutes!

But I remember his wonderful stories, his life, oh his life. It was not a long life but it was breathtaking the art he made (no, not a painting or photography or even a book) but the real art was his life, the message he gave to the world in how he lived, in his online journal that seemed like a wild fantasy or careless adventure, how he frustrated me, back here in a sensible job and commuting every day, how I missed him, but how he lived, how he embraced his time volunteering with a jaguar, how he worked with teenagers who will always remember him, how he let the force of his life, of his intent, of his light shine and how he was building a yurt…

And I think, maybe. Maybe not a tent, but maybe I can explore how I live more, (I can certainly do glamping) or a boat, a yurt, or a wigwam, maybe I can learn to be wild again, finally let go of all the things I believe I need in order to survive. Maybe I can just lie under the stars and sleep in Arizona, or in Africa.

            Maybe, maybe…

…maybe.

The beautiful thing I learned about firewalking is that you don't tell yourself that you're going to walk, you listen to your body, you feel it. And you can only really feel it when you are there. So you may walk, or you may not walk, but you can only know when you bring yourself to the fire.

I am not there yet.

This is how I stop driving myself crazy thinking about what and where and how next. I remember that I planned my Vegas, Arizona, Utah trip and it was a thing of perfection, because I listened to my heart. I remember that I met the love of my life because I listened to my heart and then rediscovered my life force in Mexico under the full moon because I listened to my heart. I experienced wonders in Japan and China and Morocco and Egypt and New York and Malibu and Iceland and Florence and more because I listened to my heart.

So my next trip? I'm not there yet. My heart wants to me write this all down first.

Shoulds – Warning Lights (It Shouldn't Bother Me When)

What I've learnt from "The Four Agreements" is that words are just symbols on a page or in your head, how we run things, why the brain thinks it's the boss (until you have a heart attack).

Anyway since my awakening I've found the word "should" really helpful because my brain throws it in every time I "should" do something. And then I tell it to fuck off. Which is great.

Now my thought process goes a lot more like this when I wake up.

Alarm goes off. "You should get up."

"Leave me alone." Set another hour on the alarm.

Zzzzzz

"Breakfast? Yeah, breakfast… and coffee." Body invites the brain in for a bit as I figure out what fruit I have and if I'm going to have both grapes and an apple. "Yeah, why not."

Then my brain starts telling me what I'm doing later in the day.

"Shut up and leave me alone until I've eaten my breakfast."

My brain is wonderful at keeping enough fruit in my fridge, keeping the gas tank at least half full and making sure there's enough money in the bank to pay the mortgage, but sometimes I need to override it – like when firewalking and I just tell it, "whatever happens it's an adventure". My brain quite likes adventures and problems, so if I get into real trouble, as I remind it, it can go nuts on problem solving, but for now it can sit on the bench and let me play.

It Is Given

Sometimes I get phrases in my head, like "I Ran Away From Home When I Was Just A Child". Like a puzzle I worry away at them, because I know there is some meaning. And I started hearing the words "It Is Given".

I'd been trying to find a way of looking at money that worked for me. (In January I tidied my house the Marie Kondo way, got rid of half my possessions and like that, years of messy living became a beautiful tidy home!) but I couldn't find the right teacher for money (maybe Alvin Hall?) Manifesting and mantras didn't feel right, all I knew was that the exact right amount of money for my Vegas trip kept showing up for me no matter what I did, so I figured I'd just trust it. Then I had two credit cards declined when I checked in to the Bellagio (one had no PIN – not usually an issue in the US but my main one had just gone out of date and I hadn't noticed).

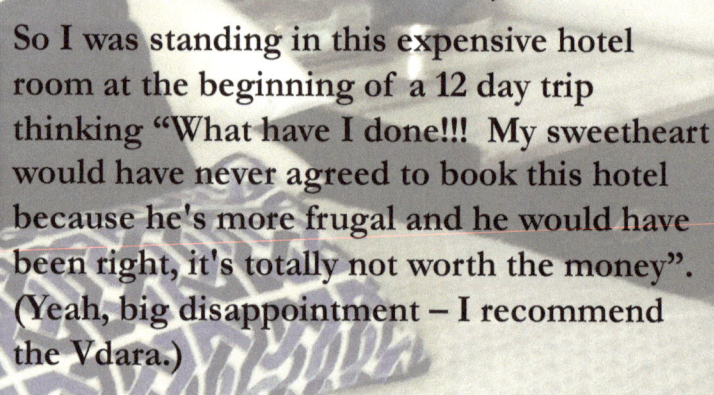

So I was standing in this expensive hotel room at the beginning of a 12 day trip thinking "What have I done!!! My sweetheart would have never agreed to book this hotel because he's more frugal and he would have been right, it's totally not worth the money". (Yeah, big disappointment – I recommend the Vdara.)

So I was hearing "It Is Given", I figured out a way to make at least one of my cards work and I was feeling pretty cocky… and then the low gas warning light came on in my car…

I pulled over and desperately started looking up gas stations on my satnav (which was being kind of iffy with the mountains and Sedona vortexes) and headed back up the road 10 miles to the gas station, praying and trying to keep the car going with the sheer force of will and unconditional love (after the whole thing with my torch battery I was being very open minded about energy). I got 10 miles up the road, only to have the satnav tell me to drive another 10 miles down a side road.

Freaking out now, I spotted a couple who had pulled over to the side of the road. I jumped out and asked them if there really was a gas station down the road, or was my satnav going to do the same thing and send me down another side road?

"Yes" said the guy, "it's about 10 minutes."

"Do you know how long you have left when the light comes on for low gas?"

"Well these newer cars are pretty good. But hang on." Which is when he took out a container and filled up my car with a quarter tank of gas. "You know, I've got four daughters and I'd hate for anything to happen to you – you got to stay safe out there."

Gratitude isn't a big enough word for how I felt. I noticed an Army insignia on his hat, "No, I'm not in the army, I'm just a husband and father."

"There's no just about that. That's everything.'

I do meet angels along the way, we are all angels, there are days when we are able to be or give exactly what is needed, days we can change or save a life...

So I'm thinking… you know I've spent pretty much all of my life worrying about money and the only times it has gone horribly wrong is when the bank or someone else makes a mistake and then I've had to ask for help and it's served me. (Oh yeah, I really wanted a snack at the retreat and I didn't have my purse with me so I asked the lady behind the table if I could give her a dollar later – it nearly killed me to ask – and every time I saw her I said, "I have your dollar right here" and she was like "You are too cute". But seriously, I cannot owe someone a dollar. The bank? I can owe them thousands, I'm cool with that.)

And then in the middle of the native American healing I felt my bear self, my "I am me and wonderful even if I sleep all winter, eat all the salmon, play for hours with a stick, growl at anyone who comes near me or my cubs…" and then I felt my eagle self, taking off, flying up to the sky and I understood the words "It Is Given".

Free will.

Free will is given.

Money?

Well, it comes and it goes, but in the natural order of things we all have enough.

So I thought about my journey. Where I got in trouble was trying to make it with the gas in my tank. I hate stopping for gas, I just want to keep on going. So like my new other new driving rule – only drink water in the car (to prevent me driving too long and spilling coffee) I added, I will fill up somewhere between half and a quarter tank of gas.

So now I'm trying to look at money like that, enough wherewithal for the next month, the next escape. It takes almost nothing to publish a book (well apart from this book because it's colour!) it's mostly time, and as a guy I met with his wife Standing On The Corner in Winslow, Arizona said "We got nothing but time, no money, but plenty of time."

Empire building is quite a faff, I'd rather just relax, take it easy and let the bare necessities of life come to me, because I usually get what I need by the time I need it (and if I don't it's usually 'cos the bank or someone else fucked up – and I get by anyway!)

Teach What You Need

Some people put the fear of God in you when you decide to put the word instructor or teacher into something you do. How long did it take me to become a Zumba Instructor? One day, or well, I've been at it nearly 6 years now, so one of those answers. What do they tell you? Well, they say, it's a good idea to get a fitness certification but in order to be a Zumba Instructor the only way to do it to go out and do it. I love that.

I have no Toltec stamp after my name (I really must go and look up the online community, but I wanted to get this out on the page before I do that) but I feel free to share what I've learned.

My therapist (and one of my greatest teachers) always reminded me that "you teach what you need", there is no shame in teaching what we have just learned. My most wonderful Maths teacher Dr Habib always asked us to come to the front and explain what we had just learned, because sometimes it's easier to learn from someone who has just got it.

I write this book for me, in case I forget how it feels to be free, in case I start to go back to old habits, in case I forget unconditional love, in case I forget myself or start to cut off pieces of myself to try and meet with someone else's approval again, if I lose the courage to think about moving out and living under the stars or in a yurt, if I forget that yes, I walked on fire and it was easy and not scary at all.

So I am teaching you what I need – and there is no shame in that.

Helping Others

Helping others can get you killed. Literally. It can also distract you from your life. It can become a drug just as much as anything else.

In my healing with Belen I asked "What do you do when everyone comes to you for advice or to tell you their sad story?" She had some ideas. They were very sensible, but I have decided to be a bear.

I work with older people and people with disabilities, some of them are lovely, some are right rat bags. Why? Because they are people.

But I shouldn't judge right? Shouldn't compare? I'll never be able to understand what they are going through or their pain? I don't want to. I am me and I control to the tip of my finger. I can't feel someone else's feelings. I can't make them feel mine. I can write, share or dance to express myself but you will never be inside my head.

I don't want to judge anyone, but I have to make distinctions (is that a fancy word for judgement?) I have to choose who to hang out with, who to buy from, who to work with, who to sleep with. I'm not here to judge you and I love you unconditionally, but I will tell you to get the hell out of my class if you are disrupting it for everyone else or for me.
I have boundaries. They are not in stone, they are in my heart.

I used to volunteer as a mentor for carers. The paperwork was endless and supervision tedious. And as a life coach and bereavement counsellor... the training was excellent and free. I saw one client for six sessions, often spaced out so it would take me three months to see one client. Sometimes I saw two at a time. I hated it. The travel, the paperwork, having to use everything inside me to try and help in a depressing, usually terminal situation and then submit my travel claims for a few pounds here and there.

When I started teaching Zumba Gold® for the over 50s I realised that most of my class were carers. In one hour I could inspire ten or twenty people, I could lift their spirits, make them glad to be alive, help them feel their feelings, cut loose and be themselves, that flash of light and love and life that is us. I loved it. And I didn't have to say goodbye. It was not six sessions spaced over 3 months, it was every week for years. I was able to connect with people, and it was a joy all round.

I taught in day centres, dementia centres, schools and clubs for people with learning disabilities, everyday schools, and to this day some of those classes will live with me as the very highest points of my life - when I was able to give something to a class, allow them to experience something - joy, life, passion, that I know in my heart no one else in the world could have done.

And some were the lowest.

Some will live with me as the days when I walked in and felt more abuse than anything else. The people who talked over, walked in front of me, belittled me, insulted me, refused to co-operate, took months to pay my tiny fee, even moments when physical contact verged on physical abuse. I kept going for the few people who loved it, who made it worth it… until they didn't. Until I realised that I wasn't serving them to my standards. I just couldn't do the job to my own satisfaction, let alone theirs.

So I quit.

You cannot help everyone. The poor are always with us.

Since my trip I've talked to many people about what I've learned. I do it because I want to, not because I feel obliged. I like that feeling. Already people are changing their lives, making that big decision, because of our conversations. I feel great joy, it's amazing what a conversation can do. But there is no way in hell I can go around the world and have that conversation with everyone – so this is what you get.

Remember how much you love yourself. Help yourself. Free yourself. Then helping others will come as naturally as breathing.

Just because you helped people before doesn't mean you have to help them again.

Some people have come to me for help, to be taught, and we have had to part ways, because somewhere along the line the help got twisted around. Helping others, whether you are paid or not, is a constantly changing agreement, especially with family. People stay in relationships, maybe even marriages because they can't let anyone down, perhaps not realising that the other person is doing the same.

When you try not to let anyone else down you end up letting yourself down.

It can be even twistier; in the words of the Eurythmics, some people want to abuse you, others want to be abused. I've seen it in fitness coaching. Some people love you to shout at them, tell them they suck, make them hurt. I do not teach my class this way. It's fucking horrible bullshit. Abuse is not love. Punishment is not love. Gentle correction of your technique, okay, if you have asked me to teach you, setting boundaries, of course, engagement, encouragement, inspiration, yes, yes, yes. But don't ask me to dominate you. Don't ask me to tell you what to wear, how to be. I am not a fashion stylist, or a dominatrix (although I can see the connection perhaps).

Help can become abuse.

"Hold people as able." This is one of the most powerful things my therapist taught me.

Yes, I want you to understand me, get free, yes, I want you to follow my moves in class, but more than anything I wish you would feel your unconditional love for yourself. I'd rather have someone dance in circles and wave whatever part of their body they feel like waving than follow me precisely trying to be me. Follow your heart and then, when we arrive at the same place and time we will know it is the right place and the right time.

There are so many lies and bullshit beliefs about helping others. So much guilt and shaming. People who try to tell you how much money to give to charity. I was one of them. It's gone. They say don't give money to someone begging on the street, they may use it on alcohol or drugs and it will only feed their habit, I say the same about the financial industry and many charities and churches that have now been exposed as corrupt and abusive. (I stopped supporting a charity for the elderly because I saw their chuggers (charity muggers) body blocking elderly people on the street to get donations.)

Sometimes doing right looks like doing wrong. There will always be people who want to shame you for not doing what they think is right. Muhammad Ali, the legendary fighter went to prison rather than fight in Vietnam. Sometimes the best way to help the world is to sit right down like a bear and say "we shall not be moved." It's sometimes so complicated that the only way to help is really, really simple. Listen to your heart.

I buy what I want from my friend and her husband, who I trust, because I know they are sending it to her family who need help. But mainly I go because she makes great food and coffee and I love hanging out with them.

Pissing People Off

I seem to be averaging pissing one person off a day (that's glib, it's more like every other day when I leave the house – today I am managing it without even leaving the house).

People don't like it when you don't do what they want, when you don't do what you used to, when you do or don't do what they do, when you tell them, no, stop talking it's my turn to talk, when you say no, I don't want to.

Feeling Worthless

How does someone else's behaviour make you feel worthless?

How does someone else's opinion make you less of a man or a woman or whatever you want to call yourself?

I read "Don't Take It Personally" in "The Four Agreements" and I tried so hard… so hard.

I didn't realise that the me I thought I was was formed from other people's opinions, which is why they hurt so much. I was being "good" so that everyone would like me, so that I would like myself. If they didn't like me, if he didn't act like he loved me, I was nothing.

I didn't take it personally when I was lying under the full moon in a rooftop pool in Mexico. I felt like life, energy, I could feel the life force inside me, and I remembered meeting him, just a life force and a body, mind and spirit – no name or occupation or 'if this then that", just a meeting of two life forces, and the energy and the spark when our hands touched.

When he didn't come to see me I felt worthless. So desperate for a crumb of love (or the appearance of love) that I would do anything, say anything, be anything to get that love. Or go the other way and hate him, hate him so hard, call him every name under the sun so it was his fault, his nasty mean spirited personality and not my fault. I threw up, I was shaking, I felt like I didn't matter, I didn't count, I was worthless.

I was alone in a hotel in Miami.

I dragged myself to a Zumba® class with Beto Perez (the creator of Zumba®).

I felt like a dish rag. We danced. With every song I remembered myself a little more, remembered how awesome and wonderful I am. Felt the joy and fun and oomph coursing through my veins.

When Beto did my favourite song I had no idea what moves he was doing, I was dancing my heart out, going crazy, being truly, madly, deeply in love with myself again.

I recovered.

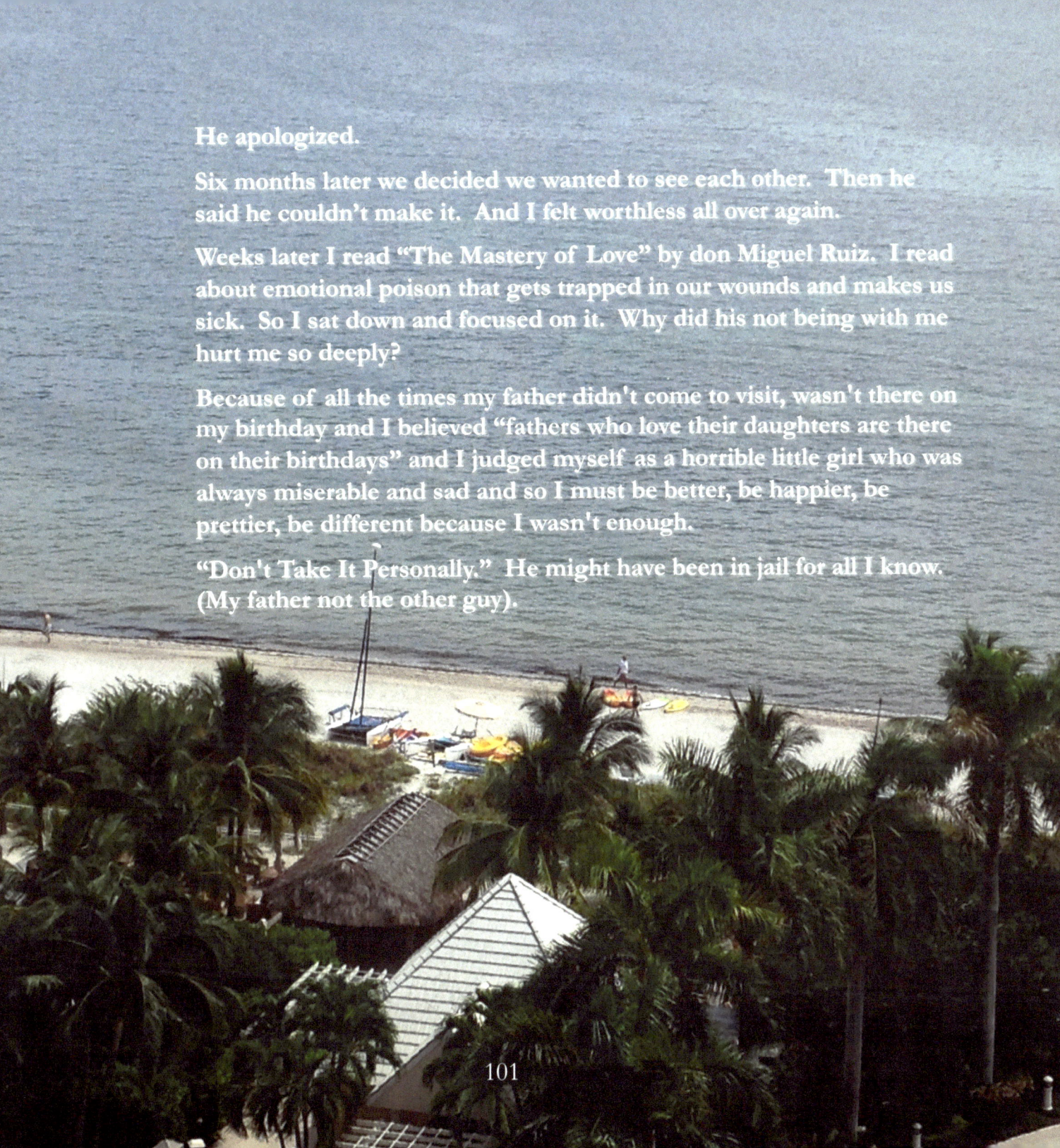

He apologized.

Six months later we decided we wanted to see each other. Then he said he couldn't make it. And I felt worthless all over again.

Weeks later I read "The Mastery of Love" by don Miguel Ruiz. I read about emotional poison that gets trapped in our wounds and makes us sick. So I sat down and focused on it. Why did his not being with me hurt me so deeply?

Because of all the times my father didn't come to visit, wasn't there on my birthday and I believed "fathers who love their daughters are there on their birthdays" and I judged myself as a horrible little girl who was always miserable and sad and so I must be better, be happier, be prettier, be different because I wasn't enough.

"Don't Take It Personally." He might have been in jail for all I know. (My father not the other guy).

Leave My Success Blocks Alone

My money blocks, my "success" blocks? I can look back now at the journey (it was about the destination by the way, I'm so glad to have got this far) and know that all those "successes" I didn't get? Well, they would have just taken me down a different path, a detour, a distraction from where I was headed.

If I'd got that job or that funding I wouldn't have made my film, which was my great love as a director – then I was done. I could have spent 30 years being "successful" without having that much freedom to tell my story and to learn from it.

If I'd stayed with that boyfriend, even the love of my life, I wouldn't be here now. So my success blocks, my money blocks were all there for a reason.

God bless them, every one.

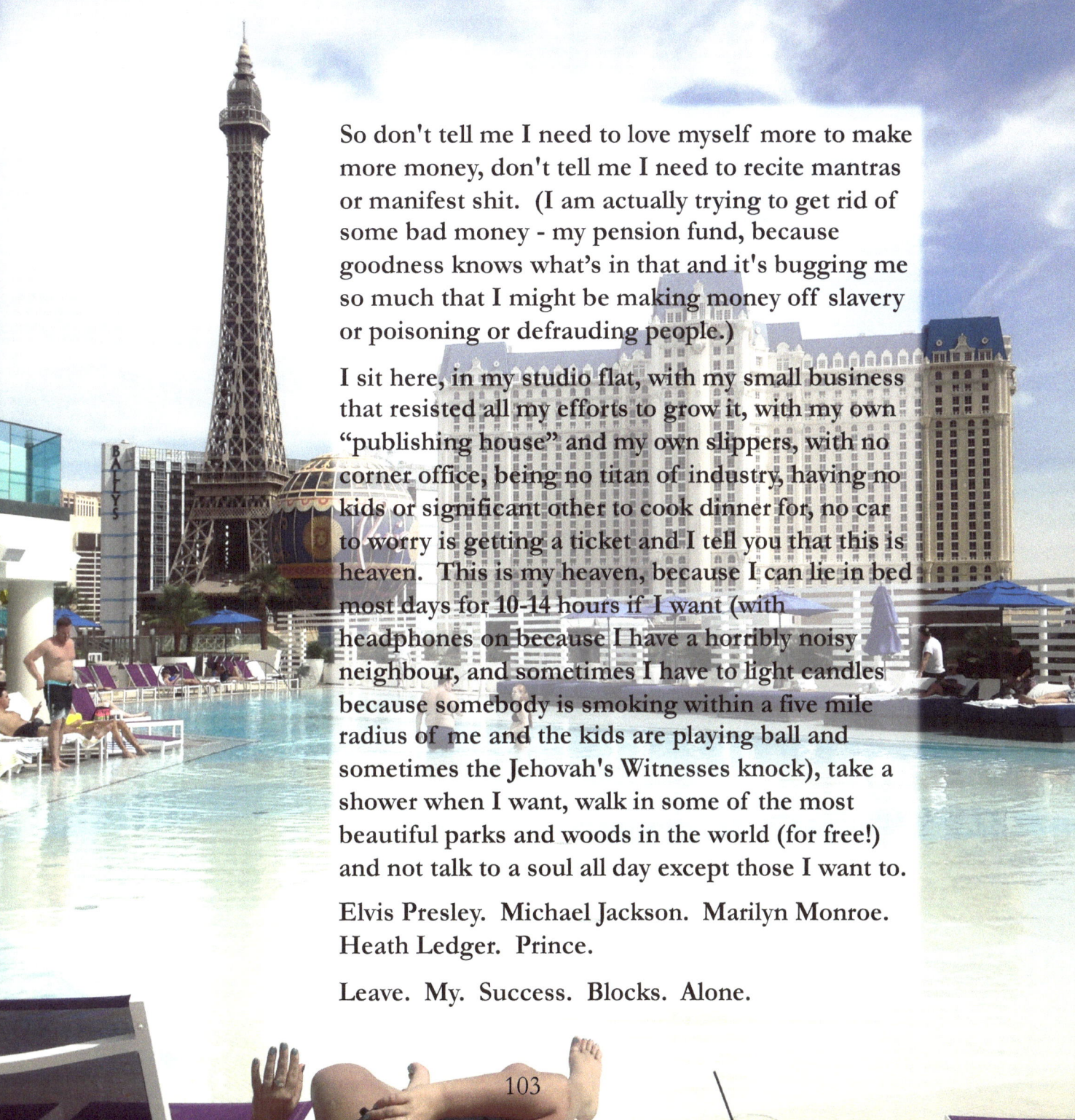

So don't tell me I need to love myself more to make more money, don't tell me I need to recite mantras or manifest shit. (I am actually trying to get rid of some bad money - my pension fund, because goodness knows what's in that and it's bugging me so much that I might be making money off slavery or poisoning or defrauding people.)

I sit here, in my studio flat, with my small business that resisted all my efforts to grow it, with my own "publishing house" and my own slippers, with no corner office, being no titan of industry, having no kids or significant other to cook dinner for, no car to worry is getting a ticket and I tell you that this is heaven. This is my heaven, because I can lie in bed most days for 10-14 hours if I want (with headphones on because I have a horribly noisy neighbour, and sometimes I have to light candles because somebody is smoking within a five mile radius of me and the kids are playing ball and sometimes the Jehovah's Witnesses knock), take a shower when I want, walk in some of the most beautiful parks and woods in the world (for free!) and not talk to a soul all day except those I want to.

Elvis Presley. Michael Jackson. Marilyn Monroe. Heath Ledger. Prince.

Leave. My. Success. Blocks. Alone.

Going Against Yourself For Love

Oh man, if going against yourself for money makes me angry, going against yourself (or should I say myself) for love makes me weep.

Don Miguel Ruiz says that the opposite of love is nothing but love. I am working on that, but I already see, looking back how much pain I have caused myself in the name of "love".

What is love?

An unseeable force that we can only feel.

And we drive ourselves crazy over it.

I know now that unconditional love runs through us and all around us. Like the sun. It is so big and amazing, like the real sun. The real sun illuminates us all, we don't pay for it, it belongs to the whole planet.

But we are nature, we change, we grow, we die, we have night time and solar eclipses and long, long winters in certain hemispheres.

And it's like those people living on the equator with more regular days turn to those people in Scandinavia with shorter days and say "Look at us, we have the sun and you don't, it loves us, not you."

So the people in Scandinavia feel bad and start drinking to numb the pain of missing the sun…

Okay, I have to leave this analogy here as I just went and did a little research online (and this was just a fantastical analogy) and there is an article about the recent "fact" that Denmark is the happiest place in the world to live. (I must admit I still prefer the idea of visiting Bhutan…)

"Sure, we Danes are very happy when it comes to answering happiness surveys – and why shouldn't we be? We take an awful lot of antidepressants! It's a funny statistic when you put the two things together but shows we're a privileged nation with ups, downs and struggles."
Adam Price, creator of "Borgen"

Let's start again. How do you domesticate an animal? A horse or a dog? By giving it food and telling it it's a good dog. When it poops on the carpet you call it a bad dog and act like you don't love it, then one of the kids goes over and gives it a few kisses because it doesn't want the dog to feel bad. And you say "Don't do that, or he'll never learn."

We treat people (and animals) as bad when they don't do what we want. We withhold our love. And we in turn start to believe that whenever we are not getting that loving attention we did something wrong.

Have you ever seen "Marley and Me?" about what they call the worst dog in the world? (They obviously never saw Cujo.) He hardly ever does what they want, they even talk about getting rid of him, but when the end comes for that dog, they're heartbroken. That dog was his own dog. And at times, when they needed someone to love them when they felt heartbroken and the dog just cuddled up with them, that dog was the best dog in the world.

"The greatest disease in the West today is not TB or leprosy; it is being unwanted, unloved, and uncared for. We can cure physical diseases with medicine, but the only cure for loneliness, despair, and hopelessness is love. There are many in the world who are dying for a piece of bread but there are many more dying for a little love. The poverty in the West is a different kind of poverty…" Mother Teresa

People reject us. Parents get so sick of their kids. Or they just get sick. And die. Friends don't want to hang around us anymore. Brothers and sisters don't want to play with us. And we think we did something wrong, we take it personally, instead of saying okay, like Marley, I'm just going to play and have fun anyway, or I'm just going to sit here and be sad because I have no one to play with, and then I'm going to go nuts and want to play with you when I see you again (and I might just chew on the furniture a bit while I'm alone).

Going Against Yourself For Happiness

So I woke up to this big misery and pain and loneliness and desperation running through me when I told myself "It's okay not to be happy." And it was awful and wonderful, waking up to my grief and my pain. Freeing. I am free to be me, to be anything, to feel anything, to know, to sleep, to cry, to talk, to write, to dance and to be a pain in the ass. Hooray.

It's like the moment you give in to flu. When you've been trying so hard to pretend you're okay "Don't worry, I'll come in to work, I can stand." And then your legs crumple and you call whoever back and you say "No. I have flu."

And you can lie back in your bed and just be.

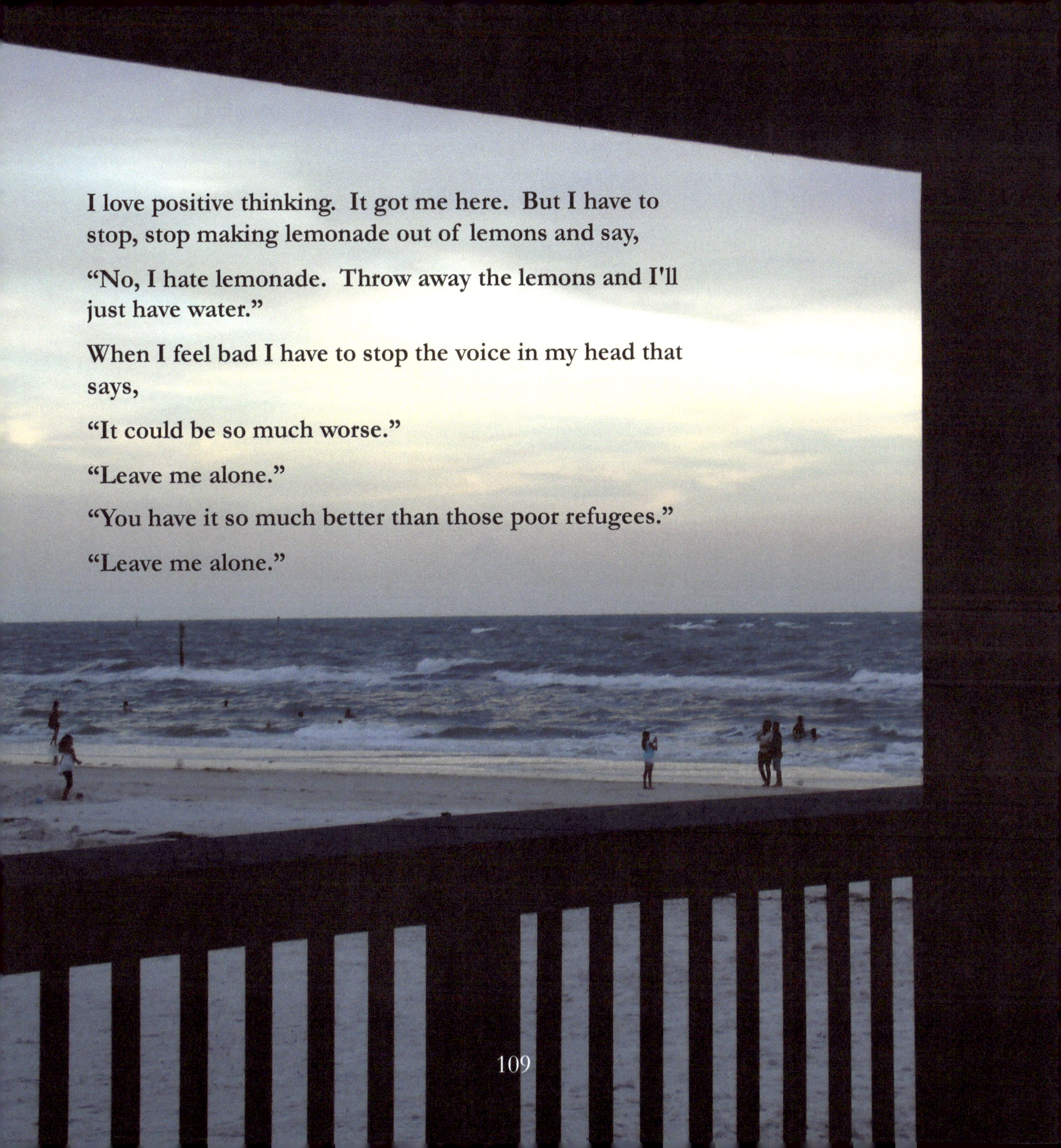

I love positive thinking. It got me here. But I have to stop, stop making lemonade out of lemons and say,

"No, I hate lemonade. Throw away the lemons and I'll just have water."

When I feel bad I have to stop the voice in my head that says,

"It could be so much worse."

"Leave me alone."

"You have it so much better than those poor refugees."

"Leave me alone."

There are things that I am deeply sad about. There is nothing to do about them. It is over. I need to heal and forgive, but really forgive, not push down or rationalize or paper over the cracks.

This is my hangover. It is not like the film "The Hangover" in that I pretty much remember most of it, but it still hurts. And I have to pay the price. The price of looking back and seeing what I did to myself. Seeing how I numbed myself in ways that are still a mystery to me. That I could separate myself, that I could cut off and not feel pieces of myself, that I could justify and rationalize things I did, things that were done to me.

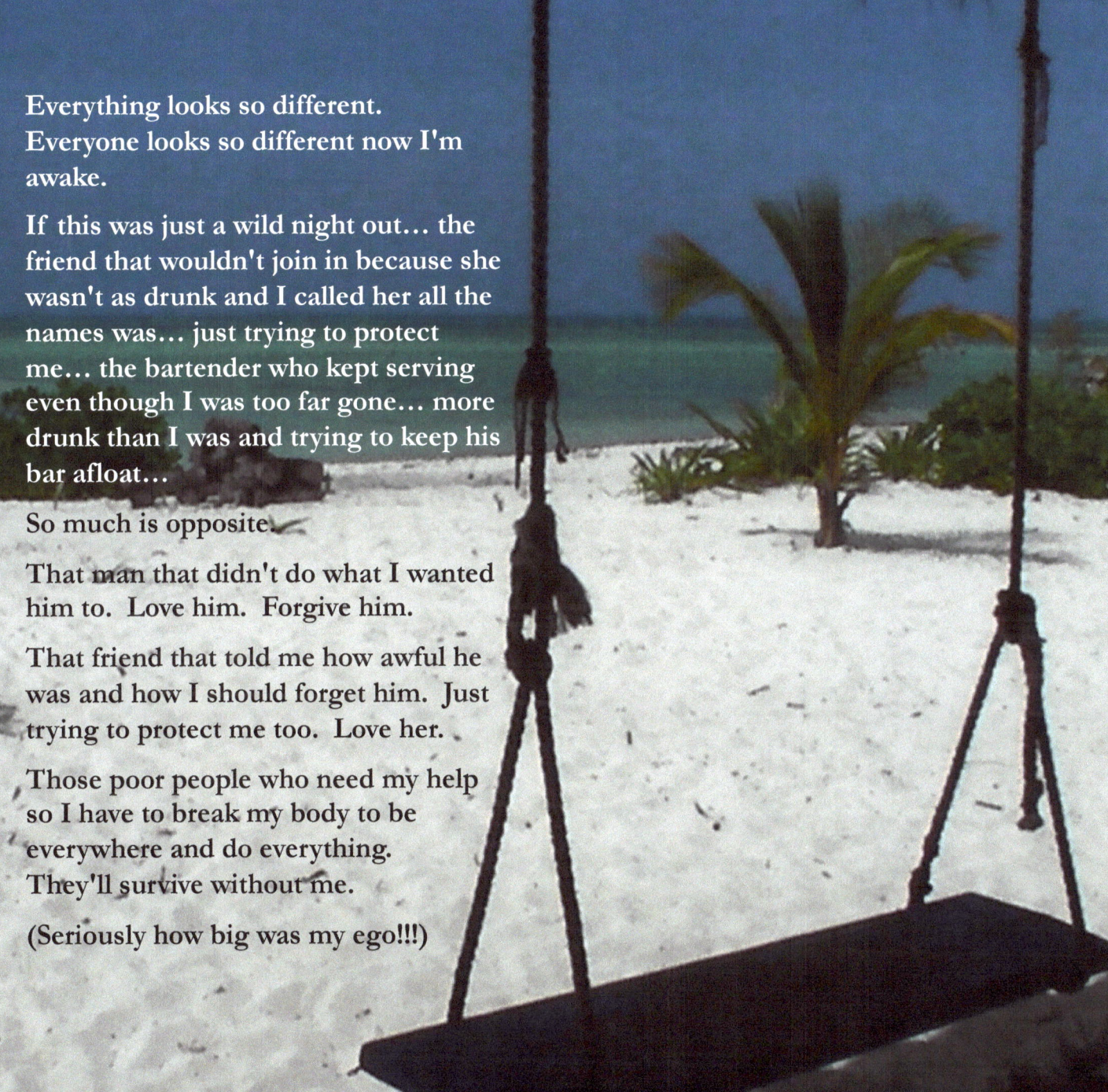

Everything looks so different. Everyone looks so different now I'm awake.

If this was just a wild night out… the friend that wouldn't join in because she wasn't as drunk and I called her all the names was… just trying to protect me… the bartender who kept serving even though I was too far gone… more drunk than I was and trying to keep his bar afloat…

So much is opposite.

That man that didn't do what I wanted him to. Love him. Forgive him.

That friend that told me how awful he was and how I should forget him. Just trying to protect me too. Love her.

Those poor people who need my help so I have to break my body to be everywhere and do everything. They'll survive without me.

(Seriously how big was my ego!!!)

Nearly six years I came up with the idea of my business Pearl Escapes. I was working in finance (forgive me). I was going to build it up until I had enough passive income (oh, what a phrase, you know what, let's call any profits I make on this book, delayed earnings, because you know writing is really not passive).

Anyway, everyone told me I couldn't leave my job and I believed them. I did an hour of yoga before I went to work, I meditated and read self-help books on the commute, I took an hour for lunch and ate lovely food, I ate more lovely food at my desk, I read two positive thinking websites every day, I did Zumba®. Then I woke up one morning with no exit plan and said "I can't do this any more."

Sometimes you have to hit rock bottom. And positive thinking is not really positive if it is just keeping you in a shitty place.

I don't want to be positive, I want to be free. Sorry, no, I take that back. I am free. I was always free. I was just very, very well trained to be happy all the fucking time.

Bad Habits – What Is Acceptable Now Will Be Illegal Tomorrow (and Vice Versa)

Even today in some countries being gay will get you sentenced to death. Being openly yourself is not an option for gay people in those countries if they are serious about staying alive, or even protecting their families.

The approved drugs of a few decades ago have been shown to be carcinogenic, deadly and are now socially unacceptable.

We are a young and arrogant society, willing to accept today's pop science and ignore thousands of years of knowing.

When we dig a little deeper into the things we denigrate now or proclaim as "traditional" we find that many of our ancestors enjoyed a freer society that took things like matrimony or homosexuality much more lightly, but took herbs and oils much more reverently. The powerful chemicals in these were known and administered with ceremony, with holistic healing of the mind, body and spirit, they were not isolated, distilled and packaged in their most potent form to be handed out, paid for… and taken lightly. (So that overenthusiastic people like me could end up in hospital by mixing essential oils!)

I recently had the honour of attending a talk by one of the world's foremost "explorers", one of the few to survive "first contact" with Amazonian tribes. These people lived for thousands of years, without modern medicine, schools, the internet, judges, courts, prisons or any of the other things we think are so essential. They don't need to study agriculture because they live easily on what the rainforest provides. When I was at school I was taught that the indigenous people slash and burn the rainforest, so it was very important that modern methods of farming were introduced to save it. What bullshit. But it was in our textbooks so we believed it. In fairness we were 13 years old.

The only large swathes of Amazon rainforest that do still exist are, according to this explorer, those belonging to tribes.

How do we separate the truth from the lies?

It starts with us, with me. Leaving behind my work when I feel a headache coming on, walking to a green space, breathing in the air and healing right then and there, without pills, without even a massage.

I need my wild time, don't you?

I don't know the truth. I am just learning my truth. I am reconsidering all my habits. What do I need? Out goes the TV, the painkillers and whenever I feel sick or fearful, instead of hiding in my flat I go out to the woods… and I feel so much better.

I can wear make up if I want, but I know I don't need it. I let go of the lie that I would be so ugly without it (isn't it funny how maybe a few hundred years ago wearing make up would have had me labeled as a witch?)

Working with love how and where I want (instead of feeling I have to help everyone or do it because I need the money). It starts with me painting the sky and eagles on my walls, with speaking my truth (and hoping no one decides to have me committed), eating what my body wants (and not a £1.99 fast food meal) and knowing that even when I am sad and grumpy I am wonderful me, and when I laugh out loud when everyone else is serious I am still beloved me, and when I tell a joke that no one understands I am still the love of my own life.

The more we can let go of our own lies, mistaken beliefs about what we need, the more we let go of our fears, the more we can hear the truth when we are asked to believe by governments and charities, like Survival International, which this explorer helped set up to protect uncontacted tribes from having to be contacted… ("Excuse me, Mr Wild Tribesman, we needed to knock on your er… leafy thing that's like a door because we need to check you actually live here and would you mind if we build a highway through here? Oh, oh I see…)

When we listen with our hearts it is harder for us to believe the lies, whether it is about rainforests and farming and highways, or damming rivers in Africa, exploration and exploitation of natural minerals, water pollution or even protecting wildlife. Because now (according to Survival International and yes, Ben Fogle) those who are passionate about protecting wildlife (yup, that includes all my many previous donations) may be funding the removal and abuse of indigenous tribes in the name of wildlife protection, just as when I was 13 years old, it was in the name of rainforest protection.

Destiny

Destiny is a stripper in Vegas (as I quipped to my native American healer). She didn't laugh. Oh well. So there's this thing called destiny, a lot of people believe in it and throw it around and I think mine is to help people feel alive and sometimes, when I haven't felt so good about myself, I've followed it thinking I was meant to help others. Now I just think it is the way I was meant to help myself (although of course that probably means it could be a pathway for others) but I realise I don't have to follow it. I can just sit right down in the road like a big old bear. If I want.

Destiny does sound a bit high and mighty so I'll just say this; save yourself first. "Physician, heal thyself." Put on your own oxygen mask first. Bring down the gazelle for yourself, the hyenas will get in there all by themselves. Get rid of the plank of wood in your own eye first.

I am escaping and leaving the door open behind me, that's enough, I don't have to carry everyone else out.

I Can Be Wrong – It's Safe To Make Mistakes

So I've been horribly bossy and bullying to myself about getting things right and I get it, when I went to school and got all As it was safe – I got rewarded, I was the teacher's pet. It was wonderful. I didn't get detention, I didn't get called out, I thought I was loved and safe.

Even if I occasionally made a big mistake (like punching another kid in the face because he smacked my money out of my hand – it wasn't me, it was my body reacting in self-defence) I got forgiven quickly and easy because "We know you're a good kid". So giving up the know-it-all, the A grades, the being perfect, Miss Hospital Corners (never made a hospital corner in my life, but I love that expression), giving up my pride and arrogance in being right, being perfect, being the teacher.

I'm working on it.

I've let go of my respect of authority and of teaching institutions, in general. But there's still a part of me that wants the pat on the head, wants the selfie with the big teacher, wants people to know I took this degree and that training.

But if I'm not trying to impress the other kids (and I never really was, I was trying to shine brightly without them noticing because you often get backlash for being top of the class)… and I'm not trying to impress the teachers because they're so big they teach thousands every day… who am I trying to impress? (Don't say my family because they were always about as interested in my academic achievements as well… they weren't.)

Just me.

I'm still just trying to impress and justify my existence to myself. Instead of a journal I make this a book and I'm trying to impress myself with what I can do.

Then I realise the swing back, the other side of the coin… the reason I never sent any of my other books to a publisher, why I hid my light under a bushel, why I have 11 books already self-published and not even my beloved knew about it (it was quite a surprise to me when I counted them) because in not submitting (and the answer is in the word, right?) I wasn't submitting my writing, my love, my art to the establishment.

I was protecting that bright blue, free corner of my life.

Which is why I kept it small, why I had to understand unconditional love and how no star can outshine another, had to be completely free and stop judging myself before I was ready to stop hiding.

Jack Vettriano. Van Gogh. Claude Monet.

We have the internet now. When these artists were able to cling to their truth, their art, despite incomprehension and damnation from the art establishment, and they had to fight so much harder – now in the age of technology and Kickstarter and Lulu and Amazon and iBooks, why on earth would I give up creative freedom for a stamp of approval and a contract? Why would I enter artistic slavery?

Writing is my love, my life and most importantly, my playground.

I am trying to be impeccable with my word (the first of The Four Agreements), checking in with myself as I finalise each page. I may make mistakes, people may take things in ways they were not intended, but as I write this and publish I know it is my best today.

I would rather give you my best today than someone else's perfection someday.

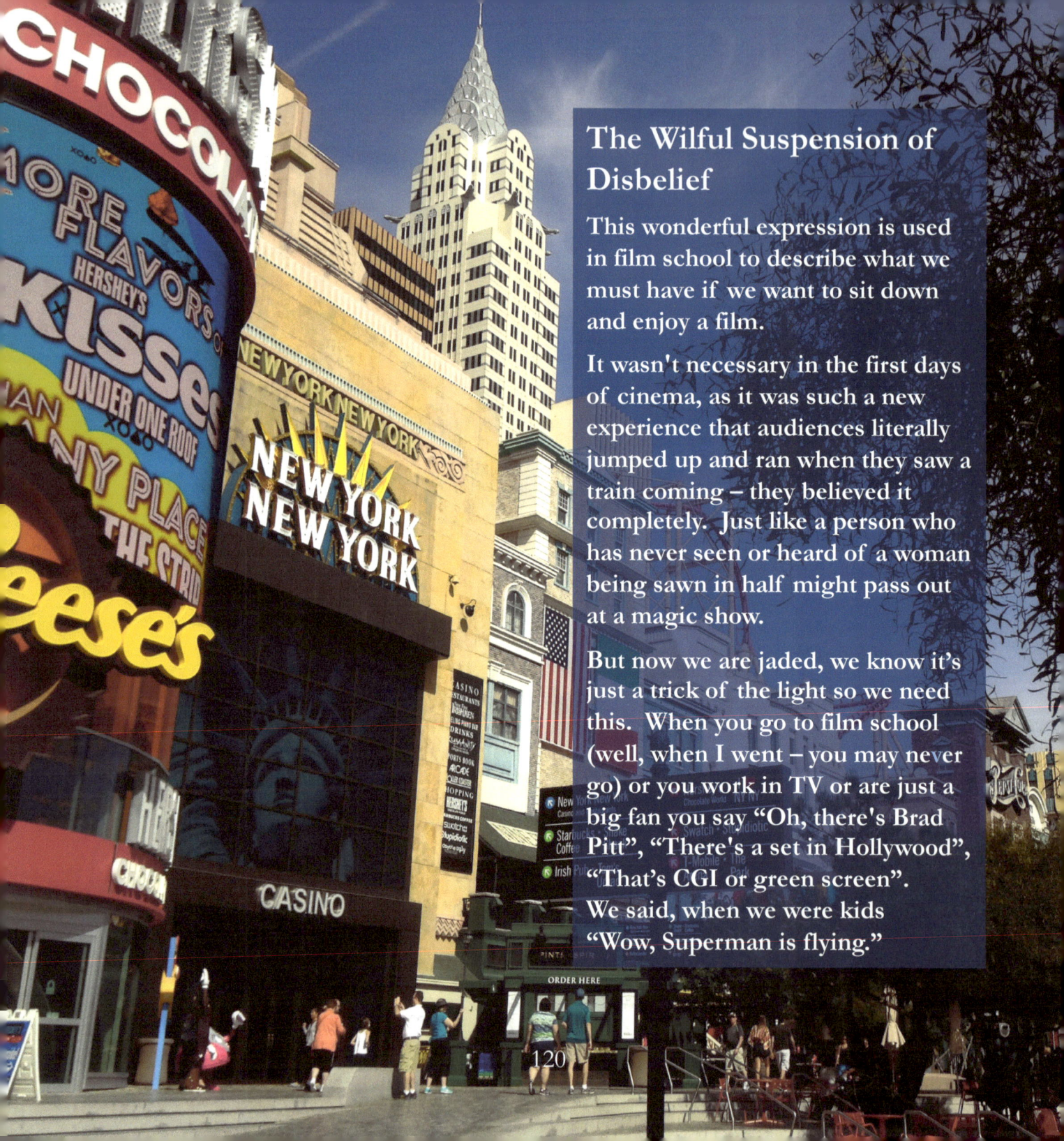

The Wilful Suspension of Disbelief

This wonderful expression is used in film school to describe what we must have if we want to sit down and enjoy a film.

It wasn't necessary in the first days of cinema, as it was such a new experience that audiences literally jumped up and ran when they saw a train coming – they believed it completely. Just like a person who has never seen or heard of a woman being sawn in half might pass out at a magic show.

But now we are jaded, we know it's just a trick of the light so we need this. When you go to film school (well, when I went – you may never go) or you work in TV or are just a big fan you say "Oh, there's Brad Pitt", "There's a set in Hollywood", "That's CGI or green screen". We said, when we were kids "Wow, Superman is flying."

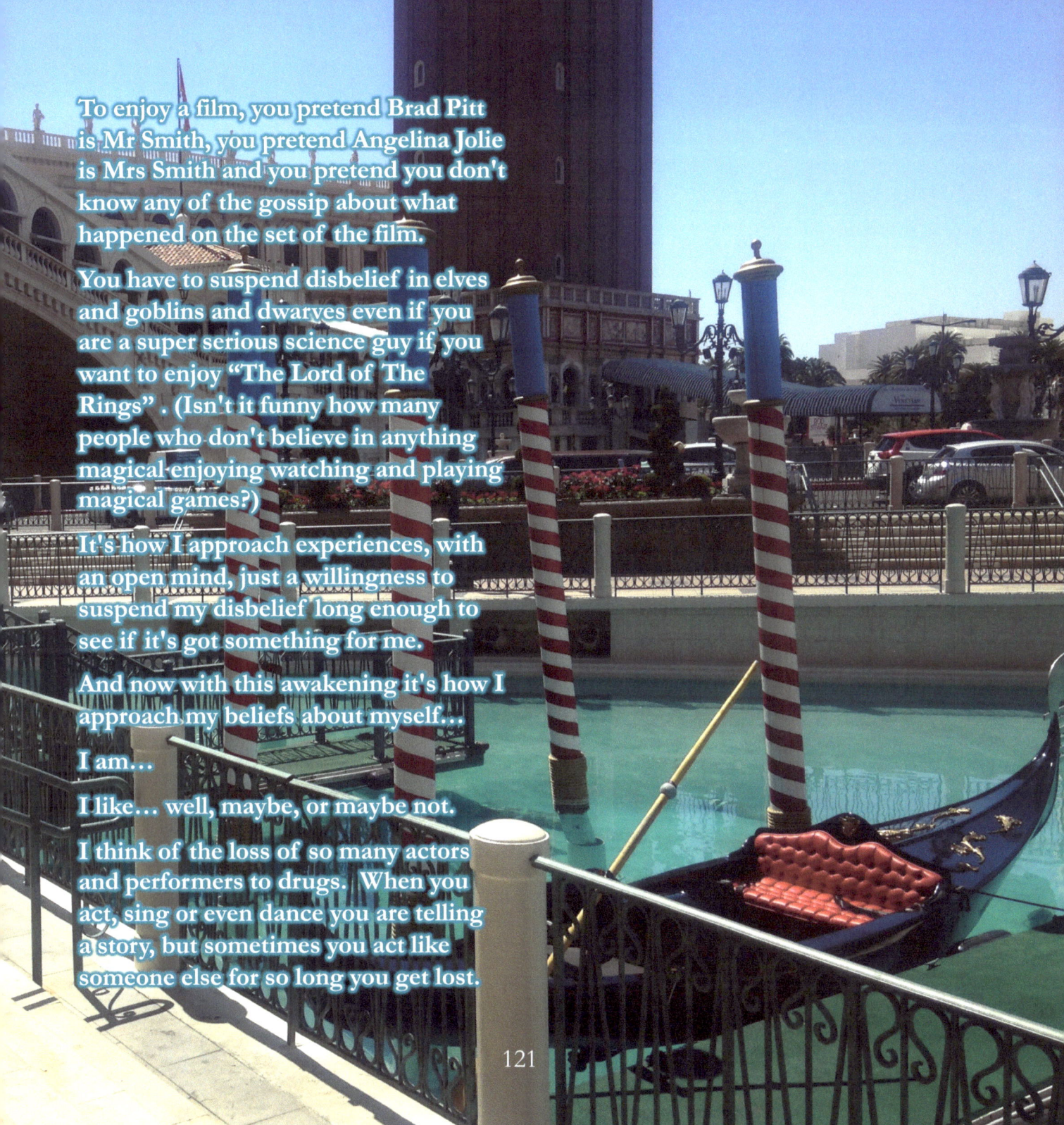

To enjoy a film, you pretend Brad Pitt is Mr Smith, you pretend Angelina Jolie is Mrs Smith and you pretend you don't know any of the gossip about what happened on the set of the film.

You have to suspend disbelief in elves and goblins and dwarves even if you are a super serious science guy if you want to enjoy "The Lord of The Rings". (Isn't it funny how many people who don't believe in anything magical enjoying watching and playing magical games?)

It's how I approach experiences, with an open mind, just a willingness to suspend my disbelief long enough to see if it's got something for me.

And now with this awakening it's how I approach my beliefs about myself…

I am…

I like… well, maybe, or maybe not.

I think of the loss of so many actors and performers to drugs. When you act, sing or even dance you are telling a story, but sometimes you act like someone else for so long you get lost.

It's why I never, ever wanted to be an actor. I was trying so hard to overcome my own acting (I thought I had succeeded) but most of us are acting and strutting and have forgotten why we started acting in the first place. And it is so painful, to have lost our true self and be caught up in an act that we have convinced ourselves is the truth.

Method acting – when we live, eat, breathe and sleep as the character. Well, who can rescue us when everyone believes the character?

Only our self.

What Do Stars Do – They Shine

Another thing I learned under the stars is that the very idea of our outshining each other is crazy. A sky where we can see one star is beautiful, but when I stood beneath a sky of millions, billions of stars it was a different understanding of the universe, it broke crappy beliefs that were holding me back into a million pieces. Each of those stars is part of the big whole, not one of those stars can outshine the heavens.

I've done so many things that against, that were too difficult, money, that took too much people told me "That's crazy, yet I did them and a lot of people warned me that cost too much out of my body, that you can't do that" and them followed me.

So I really, really hope when me, for my pleasure and others shine too. I shine bright for for fun, it lets

I Don't Care

    I don't care about your sad story – don't write it and send it to me. You should care about your own story. I don't care about that "inspirational" story you want to tell me that starts with unimaginable horror. Leave me alone. I don't want to listen to that crap. I don't want to read it on the front of the newspaper. I want to unsee it. I want the peace to deal with my own sad story and let it go and be fricking happy. Don't you want to be happy?

Forgive them, forgive yourself and be happy – that's my plan. To forgive myself for my part, cry my tears, hope to God that somewhere along the line I can find people on my wavelength who want to share all these amazing blessings in the world and not keep blaming everyone and blaming themselves.

We are fricking ALIVE, don't you get it yet?

This is a story about waking up and dealing with the hangover and remembering or maybe seeing for the first time just how cool and awesome and miraculous everything is and NEVER GOING BACK ON THE DRUGS – the drugs of numbing and self-judgment and caring what everyone thinks and whoring myself out for money or "respect" or what a boy thinks or the word success which means nothing, nothing I tell you!

This is a story about freedom, kicking the shit out of whatever is holding you back, that big bad jailor who is keeping you imprisoned without locks or keys but by the force of worrying, of fear, (and I was in there too and I don't even think that's fear). (I love Marian Keyes character Helen who says she doesn't believe in fear, she just thinks it was made up by men to get all the best jobs and shit.) …and then running for your life! Not going back and sitting around with people and talking about how bad our jailors were. Seriously. There are beaches to lay on, swim at, wild things to see and feel on your skin. Why am I still sitting here? I don't know, maybe I want to write this secret map, so if I ever wake up and there's another jailor there, telling me I can't be free, I know exactly where to kick him so I get the most time to run away.

Run for your life – it's worth it.

(And if you really feel the need to read a sad story for inspiration, read "Man's Search For Meaning" by Viktor E. Frankl.) Then escape.

Waking Others Up

One of the most powerful things I learned on the retreat in Sedona was that I control to the tip of my finger – it is not up to me to change the world, only to change my world.

But sometimes it is so hard not to jump on the desks, run through the school, slam all the doors and scream "WAKE UP!" "You are missing it! You are missing life! It is right here, right outside the door, stop studying, stop sleeping, stop drugging, stop watching TV, stop doing errands, stop everything and come outside and see this!!!"

And then they come outside and can't see it; maybe it's like a rainbow and it's gone, maybe they think you cried "Wolf". Maybe, maybe.

On my second night at the retreat I woke up around 4am again and lay there "I'm not going out to see the stars, I've seen it already, I need some sleep" and then, of course, I went and it was wonderful. And I thought, "I have to wake my room mate up". I was nervous. But I woke her anyway, I really though she might like to see it. And she did.

I am having deep conversations with people about things, sometimes it goes well, sometimes I offend. But I am awake, I am awake and I can see the stars and the moon and it's just so wonderful. So, sometimes the tip of my finger may poke someone's shoulder and I might just say "Would you like to see the stars? They're just so beautiful tonight."

Positive Thinking and Forgiving My Teachers

So one of the things I am having to try really hard not to do right now is positive thinking, it may be better than random negative thinking but right now I need to listen to my own truth.

The thing is, I am really, really, really good at positive thinking, at making myself happy, at seeing the silver lining and I need, in the words of the good don Miguel Ruiz, to "STOP".

I don't have to be happy.

I just read these things I wrote on my wall; mantras, ideas... and I'm questioning them again. Most of them are okay but there's this big one "I choose to be happy" and so I had to go find a big black marker and underneath I wrote "I choose to be myself and right now that is a bear, grrrr." It's okay to be grumpy and sleepy and any one of the seven dwarves you want to be. It's hard not to lash out when I feel like this so don't poke the bear and I, for the most part, will head out into the wild, wild woods or curl up in my cave while I reprogram my whole body, cell by cell, to be me, maybe not a butterfly, maybe not a caterpillar, I honestly don't know, but I know I'd rather be me than anyone else.

The real me has been underneath, trapped, unhappy and more than anything I don't want to go back to the imprisonment of not knowing myself and pushing my real feelings down...

But, I am not angry at others, I know most of my teachers were wrong in one way or another, this is ancient and brand new thinking, this is my oldest, oldest, deepest self and the brand new me, so I forgive them for not knowing it or not being able to teach me (maybe I just couldn't hear it).

I thought of the positive thinking author who wrote "there is no such thing as unconditional love" as I was seeing it, feeling it, having it explode all around me and inside me and I thought how sad that she died and maybe never understood this.

As much as I am putting away the fake positive thinking, the fake light… I needed it to find the real light. It's like headlights on the car that help you to drive to the Grand Canyon at dawn to see the sunrise, or the torch on my iPhone that helped me to find the darkest place at the retreat to see the stars better.

But when you get to Sedona, or wherever, you can only see the stars if you extinguish and control all that bright fake light. As I left our room to check out the stars my little torch died, it's like it knew I needed the dark, I needed the quiet to hear myself and see myself in the stars, just one of a billion, billion bright stars. My teachers were trying to tell me this, but it was just words: "I love the light for it shows me the way, I love the dark for it shows me the stars." I love the full moon too, it brought me to my beloved.

(Oh and my torch, I tried it again in Vegas before throwing it away. Worked perfectly.)

Thank goodness for my teachers who taught me through massage and music and movement because they were teaching me through touch and feeling, through my body and spirit because my mind could not let it in.

(Plus, you know, a lot of the time we didn't speak the same language!)

This journey was perfect, even the dud teachers were perfect because as I sat in their classes, their workshops I knew "Man, I could do this so much better than them, this is bullshit." Maybe that was my ego talking, because I sure as hell wasn't ready to hire a hall THAT BIG and put my picture on a banner and call myself an inspirational speaker. Now? Hell, yeah.

So it's okay that I used all the fake light, all those credit cards (accepted as real money almost everywhere – except Japan), all those ways of healing, even the duds, even the placebos, even the sugar water, even the drugs, because I made it here and I know, as I look out from what right now feels like the top of the mountain (as well as the deepest, darkest cave) that it was a fucking difficult journey, hard and beautiful and it makes me laugh to think of what I have been saying "the driving was the best and worst part of the trip" - as I drove around Nevada, Utah and Arizona, it was as if I had died and gone to heaven, but when I had my awakening, well I realized that the destination was the thing, the destination was me, the destination was freedom.

Listen To Your Heart

If you get lost, trust your instinct, trust your intuition, your body is wise, your heart knows things you can't even imagine, this is not fear, it is excitement, open your mind to all possibilities, put everything in the mix, you are good, you don't have to try to be, you are loving and loved, you don't have to earn or learn it, it is in your DNA, forget the beliefs that hurt you, remember who you are, how beautiful, perfect, loved and loving you are.

Listen with your heart, listen to your heart, it is very wise, the universe will do the rest.

You are enough, but, you know, you always were.

P.S.

After I wrote the first draft of this book I was on a high, feeling I had experienced my last true low. I felt free, I didn't care what anyone thought of me anymore. I knew myself, I wasn't scared to feel my feelings, I wasn't scared to face the world completely naked because I'd let go of everything that was holding me back, especially my pride. I knew I was no better and no worse than anyone else.

I even had the most incredible naked dream – not the one where you're naked and scared, no, I was naked and free, no house, no money, no clothes and I felt the incredible power that I was enough, that I could do anything.

Then it sort of started coming true.

My business has its ups and downs - times when I walked into class thinking "I need 9 people to show up so I can pay the mortgage tomorrow." …and when that ninth person walked in I knew there was a God (or some Mystery). (Or the day I needed £70 and someone randomly gave me a £70 tip.) I've never missed a payment on a credit card or the mortgage, even though I started a business I hadn't even defined in the middle of a recession. Something always turned up.

But my longest running centre closed the week before I left for Vegas, I got a letter from one credit card company because the hotel charged the wrong card, then another because my direct debit didn't go through. They were nice about it, sorted it all out and cancelled the fees, but every time a letter with a bank logo came I felt my blood pressure rise. I turned up to another centre where we were locked out, a few weeks later there was a flood, people weren't turning up for a million reasons, classes were cancelled because of elections and double bookings.

But I had recently discovered Kickstarter, which I thought would be a fantastic way of publishing a book if I couldn't do it through Lulu. (Guess what, I discovered I couldn't print this book through Lulu without it costing nearly £30 just for the print!)

Then I had this life changing idea - not only would I publish this book, I would tour with it! This was it, the dream that I had been too scared to own, scared to share with myself, with the world - to embrace being a writer. So I launched this incredible Kickstarter, offering not only the book but also sessions with me, the AUTHOR, and I would go all over the world to do it - you just had to fund my unseen book.

This was a great action however it turned out because, win or lose, people would actually hear about the book, plus it was a huge step for me to ask everyone for help.

The last time I asked the bank for help, spent hours explaining my financial situation, the advisor walked out back to speak to his manager, then said "We don't think we should try to put this through as they'll recalculate and may take away your overdraft."

When I asked my doctor for help because I was struggling with depression he said "No, you don't want this on your medical records, there's too much stigma about mental health." Nowadays you can go straight to the support team.

I grew up poor. I once got an I.O.U from Father Christmas. One Christmas morning there were two shiny bikes under the tree. My heart stopped. Then I read the labels. There was one for my little brother and one for my little sister. (My older brother and sister had already had their bikes. I thought it was my turn.) My heart broke.

Don Miguel Ruiz talks about Father Christmas and how the belief in him causes so much pain, because we're taught that good kids get nice presents. The best kids in the world sometimes get nothing but abuse. The documentary "The Most Fearless" is about a teenage surfer in Bangladesh who's been a street kid since she was 7 years old, because that's when she refused her parents when they wanted her to be a prostitute. I keep thinking it's a typo. But this exists in our world.

You don't feel sorry about my I.O.U. now do you? Nope.

Anyway, I went off for a cry quietly that Christmas, my older sister came to check up on me, then my mum. The big present she was going to get me had run out, but she was going to do her best to get it as soon as the January sales started. If I'd got a bike it'd have been great, but we'd have still argued, I may have fallen off, probably got bored in a few days, but it was never about the bike, it was feeling I was not good enough.

My mum juggled. There was a very specific mechanism to Christmas, a certain amount saved, a certain extra amount, buying very early or very late, hand sewn toys, charity shops, jumble sales, grandparents and aunties sending things in secret so we would have that wonderful Christmas morning. And they were wonderful (I got over the bike – bought myself a shiny new one when I was 39). My mum is the strongest person I know and I'm so blessed to have her show me what is truly important in life, if you have to juggle to do the right thing and follow your heart, well, that's what you do. Whatever material lack or problems we faced, there was never a lack of love or faith.

Being poor is not the end of the world, as long as you have a roof over your head and enough food to eat. Except… it can feel like a stigma. The poor are not trusted, the poor are charged thousands of percent of interest when those who have a good credit score are given free balance transfers. Tell us you're in financial difficulty and we'll ask you for the money we already lent you.

Ask for help and you get a social worker. Tell them you're struggling and they ask if you'd like a break. That means they'll take your kids away.

Go to the doctor with your kid who has bruises. If you're poor you get put on the at risk register. They could take your kid away.

So you're worried about your kids getting hurt, paying the rent, feeding them. But if you ask for help? Then there's a chance you'll lose your kids.

If you ask for help too much in a job? Maybe the job gets taken away.

If you already have good grades and ask questions in class it's insightful, if not it's another black mark against your name. Make a bad start in your degree and you're unlikely to get to the top of the class, because in the teacher's head you're a C student.

Yesterday I was in a bookshop, every time I spoke to someone it was shit, there was a pervading sense of cultural snobbery, elitism. It's a fucking bookshop. Books are the dissemination of knowledge, sharing experiences with the world. I don't come to a shop to be judged by an ASSISTant. I can see why bookshops are closing down. It's not because people aren't buying. I buy online because the book I want isn't on the shelf. I buy books in wellbeing shops and spas. I buy in airports because I love paperbacks. I buy eBooks because I have to read that book RIGHT NOW!

The people who come to my classes are often too scared to walk into a gym, they feel they'll be judged. They've been turned away, told by their doctor "Well, you're old, what do you expect." They've asked for help and instead they got judgment. The millions of people who bought Zumba® DVDs, well I'm guessing a lot of them wanted to work out at home so they didn't get judged by a gym or an instructor.

The Zumba® organisation trusted me to be an instructor, because they made a decision to trust everyone instead of judging them first. It changed my life.

Paypal made a business out of trusting everyone with money. There's another foreign exchange company that saw how much people were being charged to send money to poorer countries… (Want to be trusted less than a poor person? Be foreign and poor.) …so they trust people to pay just what they want (seriously, it's out there). Kickstarter trusts creative people to live up to their rewards promises.

So I tried to let go of those beliefs… That the poor are not trusted - so never admit to be being poor. The weak are taken advantage of - so never admit to weakness. I decided to ask for help, to let go of the need to be better, smarter, stronger, walk taller, act richer, be cleaner than everyone else. No more. I thought "Today I do my best, no more, no less because I am enough".

I launched my Kickstarter on Wednesday, excited, at 8am. I emailed almost everyone I'd ever met. Several of my friends pledged. I got up early on Thursday to check how many had pledged… One. Then it stopped. People told me I was inspiring, but didn't back me. On Friday I slept till 11am and got back into bed (after almost getting the energy to write FAQ on my Kickstarter page) at 5pm. On Saturday I realised I was in trouble, the d word (depression) was hovering. I taught my Zumba® class and felt cheered almost to the end when it hit me. Terribly sad stuff in my life was happening. It wasn't the Kickstarter, it was everything else. I didn't want to eat. (This, I know, is dangerous territory.)

So I stayed in the park, I ate a cheese scone and then another, because I could. I went home and meditated, why was I worried, I was free?

That night I dreamt my friend was laughing at me. "Okay" she said "you got me, I was never really your friend, I was just pretending." I got up and went to the woods. I read "The Four Agreements" and it hit me; "Don't Take It Personally". Everyone had their own shit going on, there was no blame here, no judgment, just the judgment I was making on myself. So I did a good Sunday in the woods, I hugged many, many trees, I ate lots, I bumped into friends who apologised "I'm so sorry I've been busy, I'll definitely read your email." And I told them. "I took it personally. I got all X Factor. It is inspiring, but not because I win or lose, because I took action." I was the one beating myself up.

It is so intoxicating to be lauded, so delicious to let the seed of pride grow again. "You really love me, I am so grateful." And the moment it stops it's like a drug that has been taken away. "Nobody loves me, what did I do wrong? Which PR company should I hire to spin me so everyone will buy me?"

I am the same person, with the same talents when no one or when twenty people walk into my class. When one person or a million buy the book. If my father turns up to my birthday, my lover, my friends or if I am eating cake for a month.

Life can be a popularity contest, if we want it to be. But if it is a choice between cutting myself to fit or walking in the woods by myself, I choose to hug trees.

I learned a lot from the Kickstarter, but it didn't make me any money.

I still had a roof over my head and enough to eat. Then things got crazy, I asphyxiated myself, there was a shooting in Orlando, an MP was shot and killed in England, there was the EU referendum and the big message being screamed by the newspapers and politicians was "There is not enough to go round."

In the middle of this shit storm I had one of the scariest dreams of my life. I was with my family in a clean, white, sterile place, we had been rescued, were being taken care of. And then I saw the children in my family having their lives decided for them, their most personal choices taken from them. I screamed and tried to smash up the place but nothing would break. I woke up and realised I was choosing to be safe, even though it meant giving up pieces of myself I hadn't even allowed myself to acknowledge were important.

So I put the house on the market. I asked my family for help (I've borrowed money from them for the first time in my life). I called the credit card companies (who were surprisingly helpful). The phone and TV people not so much.

I'd lost touch with that unconditional self love, so I sat right down in the park and listened and listened until I felt it again, all the way round and through me. And I understood that my ego, the impostor that thinks it's me is terrified; its desire is simple, to exist, and it will bully and lie to stay alive (and it is hard to let go of this companion, I'm fond of her). But me, my real self, the deepest heart of who I am, has but one desire and that is to explore. I know I am enough.

I may be left with nothing when I sell. I hope not. I hope I have enough to do all the things I dream of. But the things I dream of are both incredibly huge and incredibly simple; to be with the people I love, to dance, to write, to speak, to share and to explore – because, for me, these are all just other words for love.

Lots of love, Pearl x

Photo Credits

All photos by Pearl Howie excluding the following pages:

Pages 69, 92, 100, 123. These photos are by the incredible Reinaldo Medina. Thank you Reinaldo for helping me be myself even with an enormous lens pointed at me.

About the Author

I am currently a Zumba Instructor living in Wimbledon (you can Google me and come to my classes – please do). If I'm still there, of course.

For the last 6 years I've felt called to experience and write about as many escapes, particularly massage, spas and healing as I could. I believe now that this was leading me ultimately to Sedona and to Chandler, Arizona to the Thoachta healing. (Coincidentally my beloved has lived most of his life only a few miles away from there.)

I've written many books about my experiences with the hope that they will help people in some way, but I do it because I love to write, love to teach, love to share the miracles I've experienced. It also means a lot to me to help people out of pain, whether it's the torment of deciding whether to donate a kidney, supporting someone to get pain relief, helping people to understand and manage their anger, and now with this book, even before it was finished, just hearing about it has helped people to follow their hearts and do astounding things. It takes the pressure off me to do things myself and just be free to hug trees and hang out in the woods.

I may be a shaman depending on what day it is and how you choose to define the word – this is my attempt from my last book; "a shaman is someone who is aware of the importance of spirituality in healing and uses that awareness to help heal mind, body and spirit."

Other Titles by the Author

Love And The Perfect Wave

The Wee, The Wound And The Worries: My Experience Of Being A Kidney Donor

China Spa Princess – The Guide from Pearl Escapes

Hong Kong Spa Princess – The Guide from Pearl Escapes

Yangshuo Spa Princess – The Guide from Pearl Escapes

Shanghai Spa Princess – The Guide from Pearl Escapes

Huangshan Spa Princess – The Guide from Pearl Escapes

Beijing Spa Princess – The Guide from Pearl Escapes

(Also more individual location and spa guides which I am publishing now.)

Spa Breaks – The Guide from Pearl Escapes

Spa Treatments – The Guide from Pearl Escapes

Meditation for Angry People

Video

Everything To Dance For

Book References and Further Reading

The Four Agreements, The Mastery of Love – Don Miguel Ruiz (and The Fifth Agreement with Don Jose Ruiz and The Voice of Knowledge with Janet Mills)

Listening With Your Heart – Wayne Peate

The Life Changing Magic of Tidying Up – Marie Kondo

Walden – Henry David Thoreau (I'm still only halfway through.)

Grey's Anatomy – TV Series – created by Shonda Rhimes

Find Your Thing – Lucy Whittington

Man's Search For Meaning – Viktor E. Frankl

The Gifts of Imperfection, Daring Greatly and Rising Strong – Brené Brown

A Return To Love – Marianne Williamson

The Little Paris Bookshop – Nina George

Rachel's Holiday, Anybody Out There – Marian Keyes

No Mud, No Lotus – Thich Nhat Hanh

Spare Room Tycoon – James Chan

Year of Yes – Shonda Rhimes

The 4-Hour Work Week – Timothy Ferriss

The Fault In Our Stars – John Green

Anyone Can Do It – Sahar and Bobby Hashemi

www.ingramcontent.com/pod-product-compliance
Lightning Source LLC
Chambersburg PA
CBHW041123300426
44113CB00002B/37